Christoph Schalk
Jon Haley

How to Implement
The 3 Colors
of Ministry
in Your Church

D1379332

*The Pastor's Guide
for "Gift-Oriented Ministry"*

NCD Implementation Resources
Helping you apply the NCD principles
to your own ministry situation

Also Available for the Quality Characteristic "Gift-Oriented Ministry"

The 3 Colors of Ministry
> A trinitarian approach to identifying and developing your spiritual gifts. Includes: The *Three-Color Gift Test* (how to discover your God-given potential), The *Change Compass* (how to grow as a Three-Color Christian), and many practical exercises that help you apply your insights individually or as a group.

How to Study The 3 Colors of Ministry in Your Small Group
> A tool that enables small group leaders to guide their groups through the life transforming process of discovering their spiritual gifts. Provides suggestions for one, three, six, or twelve sessions.

How to Use The 3 Colors of Ministry in a Mentoring Relationship
> A tool especially designed for "gift counselors" and others who want to come alongside of other believers on a one-on-one basis to assist them in relating their gifts to corresponding tasks within the church.

For the Foundational Introduction to NCD:

Christian A. Schwarz, *Natural Church Development*
> Hardcover, 128 pages, fully illustrated.
> ISBN: 1-899638-00-5

www.churchsmart.com

www.NCD-international.org

Published by ChurchSmart Resources, St. Charles, IL 60174

© 2001 C & P Verlag, Emmelsbüll, Germany

© U.S.A. Edition: 2001 by ChurchSmart Resources
3830 Ohio Ave., St. Charles, IL 60174
1 800 253-4276
Churchsmart@compuserve.com

Edited by Kathy Haley, Christian A. Schwarz

Cover design: Heidenreich Kommunikationsdesign

ISBN: 1-889638-25-0

What are
NCD Implementation Resources?

Reading a book is not the same as applying its contents to your life. Applying it to your life is not the same as applying it to a small group. Applying it to a small group is not the same as applying it to your whole church.

NCD Implementation Resources have been designed to support you in the process of applying the proven principles of healthy churches at these various levels of church life. Eventually, there will be one basic book for each of the eight quality characteristics of Natural Church Development (*The 3 Colors of Love* for the quality characteristic "Loving Relationships," *The 3 Colors of Spirituality* for the quality characteristic "Passionate Spirituality," and so on). Each of these books will be accompanied by three implementation tools that focus on different levels of application: the individual believer, the small group, and the entire church.

You do not have to study all of the **NCD Implementation Resources** in order to start applying their concepts. You can begin with the imple-mentation level of your choice. Then, if you wish, you can move on to the other levels. The only book that is a "must-read" before using one of the implementation tools is the corresponding "3 Colors" book: which, in the case of the quality characteristic "Gift-Oriented Ministry," is *The 3 Colors of Ministry*. The basic concepts that are described there (for instance, the mean-ing of the "three colors," "color deficiencies," "gift projec-tion," "gift mix," etc.) are not repeated in the implementa-tion tools. All page references in this book relate to the basic book *The 3 Colors of Ministry* unless indicated otherwise.

You do not have to study all of the NCD Implementation Resources in order to start applying their concepts. You can begin with the implementation level of your choice.

On page 4 you will find an overview of the **NCD Implemen-tation Resources** that are available for the quality charac-teristic "gift-oriented ministry." Not only does this overview give you a "bird's eye view" of the four NCD books for this quality characteristic, but it also briefly states what the goal of each one is, for whom it might be most helpful, and what you might expect as a result of using it.

NCD Implementation Resources are about helping you focus your energies where they might do the most good in the way that they might do the most good. Whether that needs to take place at one level of church life or another, you will find an **NCD Implementation Resource** to help.

**Natural Church Development:
A different approach
...for different results.**

Different Tools for
Different Levels of Implementation

Tool	Goal	For Whom?	Natural Results
The basic book: *The 3 Colors of Ministry*	• To help believers discover their spiritual gifts. • To help people identify their personal starting point for growth in the balanced use of their spiritual gifts.	• The individual Christian. • If working with a small group, all group members. • If working with an entire church, all church members.	• Christians will be able to identify which gifts they do and do not have. • They will be able to identify with one of the six starting points and develop a personal growth plan.
Level 1 Implementation: *How to Use The 3 Colors of Ministry in a Mentoring Relationship* (The Mentor's Guide)	• To enable those who desire to help other believers relate their gifts to specific tasks. • To be a "gift counseling" tool within a church that is implementing the gift-oriented ministry approach.	• Anyone who wants to share *The 3 Colors of Ministry* concepts with another individual (friend, small group or church member, etc.). • All church "gift counselors."	• Christians will receive personal help in implementing the concepts found in *The 3 Colors of Ministry*. • A multiplying network of gift counselors will be established in the church.
Level 2 Implementation: *How to Study The 3 Colors of Ministry in Your Small Group* (The Group Leader's Guide)	• To provide guidelines for a small group discovery process. • To deal with spiritual gifts and starting points in the most "natural" setting: the small group.	• All group leaders (and co-leaders) that are involved in the gift-oriented ministry implementation process.	• Group participants will help each other in their growth process. • They will experience the life-transforming relevance of the Bible's teaching on the subject of spiritual gifts.
Level 3 Implementation: *How to Implement The 3 Colors of Ministry in Your Church* (The Pastor's Guide)	• To provide guidelines for implementing balanced, gift-oriented ministry throughout an entire church body. • To supply computer software for obtaining congregational results.	• Those leaders in the church that are responsible for supervising the implementation process (e.g. pastor, elders, ministry coordinator, etc.).	• The church will increase its quality in the area of gift-oriented ministry. • It will experience the positive effects of this growth process in other areas of church life.

Contents of
This Book

Table of
Contents

Surveying the Implementation Process

An idea. That's what you have. A vision of a better version of your church. A church shaped by the pattern that God himself designed for it. A pattern structured by the spiritual gifts he has given your church. But how do you turn that vision into reality? This chapter will help you begin thinking through all that is involved in an implementation process for balanced, gift-oriented ministry. It will also further acquaint you with the focus of the NCD Implementation Resources and the practical tools that they offer.

Why an Implementation Guide for Spiritual Gifts?

Many churches know that employing the spiritual gifts present in a congregation is foundational to healthy ministry. They consider this a biblical "given." Many also know that a large percentage of believers need help in discerning what their spiritual gifts are. Therefore, they have invested a good amount of time in helping believers identify their gifts.

It is tragic, however, that many have not moved beyond gift discovery. Often it is assumed that once one's gifts have been identified, finding a ministry that matches, getting started in that ministry, and developing one's skill while ministering will come automatically. Even those who do not make this assumption will not know what to do once spiritual gifts have been identified.

Often it is assumed that once one's gifts have have been identified, finding a ministry, getting started in it, and developing one's potential while ministering will come automatically.

Moving Beyond Mere Gift Discovery

The *NCD Implementation Resources* for the quality characteristic "gift-oriented ministry" have been designed to help your congregation move beyond mere gift discovery. We hope to show you how a congregation's approach to ministry can become more gift-oriented in actual practice. This process will result in a congregation that functions as a body, like the New Testament describes.

Take a moment to consider the following questions: Currently, in what ways can the members of your church minister with their various gifts? Is the uniqueness of each individual appreciated, or overlooked? Are some volunteers expected to be "supermen"? How many individual members know what their spiritual gifts are? Do those individuals minister according to their gifts?

In many churches, volunteers are placed in the wrong ministries. In the end, they are more frustrated, less motivated, and experience little joy in ministry. As is often the case among the leaders of the church, their spiritual passion slowly dies. They may not feel comfortable in their positions because their spiritual gifts do not match their tasks. The church may lack vision because the leaders do not have the gift of leadership. Worship services are boring because members with appropriate gifting are not contributing. Small groups are dying because they are not being led by those who have the gift of shepherding. People share their faith in confrontational ways, because they feel pressured to do so, even though they don't have the gift of evangelism. Ultimately, the entire ministry of a church is affected because gift orientation is disregarded.

Gift-oriented ministry implies that the pivotal criterion for one's ministry within the church is his or her gift mix, which results in ministry that corresponds with God's ministry plan for the church. Becoming a gift-oriented church implies the consistent application of this principle throughout the church. The entire congregation needs to be included in this approach in order to reflect God's image of the body of Christ.

Bringing Positive Balance to the Use of Spiritual Gifts

Balance is a key element of the NCD philosophy at every level. For example, at the level of the quality characteristics, the NCD approach emphasizes that *all* eight characteristics must be present, and that no single characteristic can be expected to produce miracles for the church. Balance is also a key element of the minimum factor strategy, since what it seeks to accomplish is to bring weak characteristics into balance with strong characteristics.

But it is not just *any* kind of balance that NCD advocates. One could hardly consider having equally *underdeveloped* characteristics a desirable condition! NCD seeks to foster *positive* balance; *strong* equilibrium.

In an analogous fashion, the three-color paradigm seeks to bring positive balance to gift-oriented ministry. At an individual level, some believers may know what their gifts are, but may be using them in an untrained way in their ministry commitments. That would not be balanced. At the church level, nearly every member could be involved in the ministries for which they are gifted, but the church might discover that these gifts are overwhelmingly in the "red" area, while many of the gifts in the "latent" category are in the "blue" and "green" areas. Because the church has not valued those areas adequately, the development of those gifts has never been encouraged.

It is not just any kind of balance that NCD advocates. NCD seeks to foster positive balance.

This guide will help you strive for balance in your gift-oriented ministry implementation—radically positive, radically three-colored balance!

The Tools
at Your Disposal

Y ou may wonder why there are several implementation resources, and not just one. Each tool serves a different purpose and is to be used by a different key leader in the church. The following resources comprise the *NCD Implementation Resources* for *The 3 Colors of Ministry.*

How to Implement The 3 Colors of Ministry in Your Church

The book you are reading right now is designed to help pastors and church leaders get the most out of *The 3 Colors of Ministry* in their churches. It is a step-by-step process for becoming a more gift-oriented church. It will guide you in introducing, carrying out, and facilitating ministry that is structured according to spiritual gifting.

Each tool serves a different purpose and is to be used by a different key leader in the your church.

This book should be read by the Senior Pastor, the Ministry Coordinator in charge of implementation, and whoever else will have a decisive role in deciding whether or not to proceed with this approach to gift-oriented ministry in your church. Once you have launched the implementation process, you might want to keep this book available for accessing the worksheets it contains.

The 3 Colors of Ministry CD-ROM

How to Implement the 3 Colors of Ministry in Your Church comes with a CD-ROM that includes all the diagrams and cartoons from *The 3 Colors of Ministry* for use in teaching. It also includes software to help you analyze your church's composite *Change Compass* and *Three-Color Gift Test* results.

Consider making the CD-ROM available to your seminar leaders early on in the process so that they can prepare their overhead transparencies, Power Point presentations, or handouts with the benefit of the graphics and cartoons that are included. These are available as low and high-resolution TIF images that will project and print well.

The software program included on the disk is designed to help you take the individual test results of your members and merge them into composite views of your church's tendencies. They can provide you with unique perspectives on the question of balance in your church's ministry style and gifting. (See pages 14-18 and 48-54 for more on the potential value of these results in your implementation efforts.)

How to Study The 3 Colors of Ministry in Your Small Group

This book has been developed for small group leaders. Among other things, they will find practical suggestions for conducting anywhere from one to twelve units of study on spiritual gifts. They will discover a process that will enable their group members to learn about their spiritual gifts and their personal areas for growth.

This is an especially valuable tool since the small group experience is unique among the learning environments you can offer the members of your church. For example, while *The 3 Colors of Ministry* has two tests that have been developed with a great deal of care, they are not considered the "be all and end all" of gift discovery. They are supplementary to a *process* of gift discovery. For that matter, in the unlikely event that a believer had to choose between participating in a gift-discovery process or taking the gift test, we would encourage him or her to participate in a discovery process without hesitation!

That is why the longer-term, small group experience is so important. It is an ideal setting for the sort of personal exploration of gifting that cannot happen by simply taking the test in isolation or merely attending a seminar. It is the natural environment for people who know and care about a person, to interact with him or her about their spiritual gifts. It is an ideal setting for others to confirm whether or not the person really does have the gifts they think they have.

Group members will also spend a good deal of time discussing *how* they engage in ministry. Are they "Thomas," "Martha," or "Mary" types? What are their strengths and weaknesses? In the safety of a caring group, one can process this subject with a far greater degree of transparency than might be the case either in a seminar or with a gift counselor whom one may or may not know that well.

How to Use The 3 Colors of Ministry in a Mentoring Relationship

A core objective of the entire gift-oriented ministry approach is that church members discover their spiritual gifts. It is crucial, however, not to stop with the discovery of the individual gifts, but to wisely apply those gifts to ministries that correspond with them.

A mentor or counselor can help build that most important bridge between spiritual gift discovery and specific ministries in the church. It has been our experience that only a few of the people who discover their gifts actually get involved in corresponding ministries without the input and advice of someone else. That is why we believe that the majority of Christians can find their place in meaningful ministry if they have personal assistance to help them think through their spiritual gifts, interests, skills, and other factors. This booklet provides direction for this kind of one-on-one ministry. It helps believers counsel others in the wise investment of their spiritual gifts in church-edifying ministry.

In the unlikely event that a believer had to choose between participating in a gift-discovery process or taking the gift test, we would encourage him or her to participate in a process without hesitation!

Coming to Terms with Your Implementation Starting Point

We must emphasize that you can identify your spiritual gifts and even apply them in some ministry on your own. To a certain degree, this can work with or without the support of the local church leadership. However, if an entire congregation is to become gift-oriented in the way it does ministry, then the pastor and the entire leadership of the church needs to be convinced of the validity of this approach and its impact on church life.

It does not matter if you are a pastor or other leader in your church, your implementation role depends on your spiritual gifts.

Neither the pastor nor the church leaders need to be the ones who do everything in this process. But, without the official support of the leadership, it is impossible that the whole congregation will function in a gift-oriented way, thus experiencing what the body of Christ is all about.

What are Your Spiritual Gifts?

There are two prerequisites for using this implementation resource. First, you must have confirmed your spiritual gifts and familiarized yourself with the *Three-Color Gift Test* and the *Change Compass* in experience as well as theory. If you have not yet done this, then your first step is to take the tests and begin applying and developing your gifts. You cannot convince others of something you have not experienced yourself!

Second, you must clarify what your role in the implementation of gift-oriented ministry in your church will be. It does not matter if you are a pastor or other leader in your church, your role should be determined on the basis of your spiritual gifts. If your gifting includes the gifts of organization, leadership, teaching, or wisdom, you might be the one to coordinate this implementation process. If you have the gifts of wisdom, counseling, or discernment, you might consider becoming a gift counselor. You need to discern if your task is to initiate the process, to carry it out, or just to support it indirectly. If you are the pastor, you should delegate the various tasks to individuals with the appropriate gifts. It is particularly important to find someone who will be in charge of gift counseling. You will find more information on this in the section titled, "Find and Train Gift Counselors" (page 30).

Where Does Your Church Stand?

What does your church think about the gift-oriented approach to ministry? Is it new and unknown? Do frustrating experiences from the past need to be overcome? Do you expect opposition? Is the gift-oriented approach going to be embraced, or resisted?

If the concept of gift-oriented ministry is new to your church, you have the opportunity to introduce it in a fresh and non-threatening way. Your enthusiasm about this approach will be contagious. The following section offers suggestions for communicating the vision of a church that ministers according to the gifting God has given it. This advice will also be useful if you face opposition in your church that is based on past experiences with gift-discovery processes that have not been adequately consistent or balanced. In this case, you need to stress the uniqueness of this approach compared to what might have been done in the past. Not only will spiritual gifts be discovered, but also an infrastructure will be created that will help individuals find their specific place in the church and minister in a balanced way.

In the face of prejudice and opposition, emphasize that it is up to the individual church member to decide how involved he or she will be in the process. Some people suspect that a gift-oriented infrastructure will give the leadership more control over the church members and their ministries. This is not true. The infrastructure is set up to serve and benefit the church and its members.

What is Your Church's Background?

The NCD Implementation Resources have been consciously developed for all kinds of churches. The concepts and principles presented in these tools should work for any type of church if the pastor and church leadership are behind it.

In the implementation steps, conscious attention is given to the possibility that you may need to make specific adjustments based on the background of your church. For instance, in the section titled, "Special Emphases" (pages 23-24) attention is given to the possibility that your church may need to think through the list of spiritual gifts with which you wish to work based on your particular theological convictions.

Once again, it should be stated that NCD seeks to encourage the individualization of universally applicable principles, not the reproduction of specific programs. However, it is in the nature of any implementation procedure, that the more specific it becomes, and thus the more "practical" it becomes in the sense of "how-to" steps, the more model-oriented it also becomes. We would encourage you to stay focused on the principles. Should some suggestion not be appropriate for your particular congregation, find another way to do it.

We would encourage you to stay focused on the principles. Should some suggestion not be appropriate for your particular congregation, find another way to do it.

Three-Color Christians in Three-Color Churches

The three-color scheme found in the NCD Discipleship Resources is guided by the theological insight that God has revealed himself to humanity in a threefold way. These revelations have many practical implications for the way that we experience God and the way that we live the Christian life at the personal, as well as the corporate, level.

Balance: The Intention of the Three Colors

The three colors are intended to be a conceptual tool that encourages us to bring balance to the way we relate to the Triune God and the way we live the Christian life. For instance, the booklet *The Threefold Art of Experiencing God* is directed primarily at bringing balance to our theological orientation (charismatic, liberal, evangelical) and avoiding their chief dangers (spiritualism, syncretism, dogmatism). In *The 3 Colors of Ministry*, it is aimed at bringing balance to the way we engage in ministry (power, wisdom, commitment), and, to some extent, even the ministries themselves in which we engage ("blue" gifts, "green" gifts, and "red" gifts).

> *The three colors are intended to be a conceptual tool that encourages us to bring balance to the way we relate to the Triune God and the way we live the Christian life.*

What is a Three-Color Christian?

When we speak of Three-Color Christians, then, we must keep this perspective clearly in mind. The three colors are a conceptual tool to help us encourage this sort of "trinitarian" balance with reference to some specific area of personal discipleship. Consequently, depending on which area of the Christian experience is being addressed, the answer will vary.

In the case of *The 3 Colors of Ministry* implementation tools, this conceptual framework is applied to the area of spiritual gifts. And it is applied in one way at the individual level: namely, how one engages in ministry. Is there balance between power, wisdom, and commitment, or does one's ministry involvement tend more in one direction than another? In a sense, we are applying a "minimum factor strategy" at the individual level with reference to the use of spiritual gifts. In what way does this particular Christian most need to grow in the exercise of his or her spiritual gifts at this particular point in time?

What is a Three-Color Church?

When we apply the three-colors conceptual framework to the church in the area of spiritual gifts, we likewise pursue the question of balance. However, at the church level, this application works out in two ways.

First, as with the individual believer, we may ask if a church as a whole is balanced with reference to the terms wisdom, power, and commitment. For example, a church that is predominately commitment-oriented (red area) might be one in which members are motivated by guilt. On the other hand, it could simply indicate that the concept of structuring ministry according to gifts has not been taught or implemented adequately. Consequently, people are serving faithfully in areas that don't fit their gifting.

Second, at the level of the whole church the three-colors idea might be helpful in assessing the distribution of the spiritual gifts that are present in your church. The gift categorization given in *The 3 Colors of Ministry* can be very insightful for discovering certain tendencies that exist in your church.

Obviously, what you decide to do with this information is up to you. You might be convinced that being a predominately "blue"-gifted church is exactly what God desires of you as a congregation. On the other hand, you might determine that this reflects an imbalance in your church's teaching emphases. We would encourage you to consider whether or not growing in some of the other gift areas is something that God would desire for your church. God may well have more in store for your congregation than you have considered so far.

Personal and Corporate Balance

Our desire is to see individual believers using their spiritual gifts wisely in committed and spirit-empowered service in the church.

By now it should be apparent that when we speak of Three-Color Christians in Three-Color churches, we are essentially pursuing balance at both the personal and corporate levels. Our desire is to see individual believers using their spiritual gifts wisely in committed and spirit-empowered service in the church. But this is not all we desire. Our international research indicates that this kind of service should characterize the ministry of the entire church. Consequently, we want to see this permeate the entire congregation. It should not merely be the isolated experience of a few believers. It ought to be a well-developed characteristic of the whole church.

Bringing Greater Balance to Your Implementation

If you are familiar with Natural Church Development, you know that the eight "quality characteristics" have to do with the elements that every healthy church needs to have. They answer the question, "*What should we do?*" The "minimum factor strategy" responds to the question, "*When* should we do it?" It suggests that a church should give priority to strengthening those areas of church life that are least developed at the current time. The "biotic principles" answer the question "*How* should we do it?" They find their inspiration in the way the created order gets high output from minimal input. Applied to the church these principles function as decision-making guidelines for doing ministry as effectively as possible. (For more information on these concepts, see *Natural Church Development*.)

A Deeper Look into the Quality Characteristics

The NCD Discipleship Resources are designed to help you take these general concepts and apply them to your church. However, the addition of the three-colors scheme provides an additional perspective. It is a perspective that can help you fine tune the process of implementation. If your church wants to focus its energy on a certain quality characteristic (for instance, gift-oriented ministry), the three-colors scheme helps you to identify some of the crucial points to work on *within* that area. It is a deeper look into the quality characteristic. Furthermore, the three-colors framework can help you address these points in a balanced way. It takes the general quality characteristic under consideration, identifies some of the key elements within it, and then deliberately seeks to make sure that none of those key elements gets ignored in the implementation process.

Taking the time for a thorough analysis of your church-wide results and planning deliberately in light of those results could revolutionize your congregation in some very positive ways.

Discovering Composite Color Blends

There are two tools in *The 3 Colors of Ministry* that can help you identify your church's "color blend" in the two areas mentioned on the previous pages. These are the *Change Compass* and the *Three-Color Gift Test*. They can be profitably used to gain further insight as to where your church as a whole is relative to these items.

At some point in the implementation process (we have placed it at Step 8), you can gather the results of all the members of your church (or a representative portion), and combine those results in a composite whole. The software program on the CD-ROM has been designed to help you do this.

The purpose of such an activity is to see if there are ways to enhance the balance of your church's ministry, both in terms of *how* it does ministry, and *what* ministry it does. It should be readily apparent that taking this step seriously could have far-reaching consequences on the life of the church!

It is quite probable that some of these changes will already be occurring naturally, as you work your way through the implementation steps. New ministries will be suggesting themselves, and existing ministries will begin to be done in a more gift-oriented way. Nevertheless, taking the time for a thorough analysis of your church-wide results and planning deliberately in light of those results, could revolutionize your congregation in some very positive ways.

Adapt as Needed, but Don't Lose Balance

As you work your way through the implementation process for your church we would encourage you to adapt the implementation steps to your ministry situation as much as needed to contextualize them. At the same time, we would encourage you to be careful about adapting steps in ways that create imbalance in the implementation process. For example, the following approaches would "short-circuit" your efforts:

- Helping people identify their gifts, but then leaving them to use their own criteria exclusively for determining how their gifts will be employed.

- Helping people identify their gifts, but then encouraging them to use them in the church in "spontaneous" ways (i.e., without planning).

- Helping people identify their gifts, but not helping them develop their gifts further.

- Assuming that all those who have a "title" or official "job" in the church have the necessary gifting to carry it out.

We would encourage you to be careful about adapting steps in ways that create imbalance in the implementation process.

- Helping people identify their gifts and relating those gifts to concrete tasks in the church, but then robbing them of the freedom to exercise their gift by micro-managing their participation in ministry.

- Determining ahead of time (based on a church strategy or a strong leader's preferences) which ministries the church will have, and then only allowing people to use their gifts in those ministries.

- Only helping the church *leaders* identify and develop their gifts, since they are the only ones who will really be doing ministry anyway.

- Doing a three-color analysis, but then exclusively picking out one color (your favorite one) and presenting it as a "universal key."

On the other hand, adaptations that keep the following values would likely maintain a healthy implementation balance:

- Establishing a plan to help people identify, use, and mature their spiritual gifts.
- Being willing to let ministries die that cannot be "staffed" by believers with the necessary gifts.
- Periodically encouraging all church members to reassess their gift mix to see if they are growing in already existing areas or are being enabled in new areas.
- Periodically re-evaluating all ministries to see if they are truly the most beneficial ways your church can stimulate the use of the corresponding spiritual gifts.
- Periodically encouraging the members of your church to suggest new ministries that would give them outlets for new or under-utilized gifts.
- Periodically having the church leadership evaluate whether they are functioning according to their gifts or have "picked up" some tasks that don't really correspond to them just because "someone had to do it." (Caution: Here, as in other areas, the distinction between spiritual gifts and "universal Christian responsibilities" needs to be born in mind.)
- Routinely analyzing the color blend of your church and striving to bring greater balance to all areas of ministry.

Launching the Implementation Process

Change happens best (and least traumatically!) when it is intentionally led by means of a well-thought-out and well-executed plan. This chapter offers the first part of such a plan. Should you wish to adapt something to suit your particular situation, this conceptual framework will help you make sure that you don't forget anything important in the process.

Step 1: Gain the Support of Your Entire Leadership Team

A fast-moving rowboat approached a flock of ducks unnoticed. The ducks kept swimming, unflustered. Finally, one of the ducks became aware of it and immediately changed its course. Most of the flock followed, but the leader was still oblivious. The boat passed between the flock and the leader. At this point, the leader noticed that the flock was no longer following him. What did he do? He stretched out his wings, rose out of the water, flew a short distance, and landed at the head of the flock again.

Not everyone will be eager to get involved in this process of change, unless they are convinced that it is absolutely necessary. Therefore, it is essential to ensure receptiveness among the leadership

Sometimes church leadership is more like this flock of ducks than we would wish! Ideally, the leaders have a vision and the flock follows. Guaranteeing that this will happen, however, takes more than vision. It takes skill and dedication.

Therefore, before launching into such an ambitious undertaking as leading your church toward a consistently gift-oriented way of doing ministry, it is important to gain the support of your church leaders. The entire flock needs to swim together in one direction. You, as the pastor (or the leader in charge of implementation), should not find yourself alone. You need the full support of your leadership team for such an ambitious undertaking.

Who are Your Key Leaders?

Consider carefully who could help carry out the implementation of gift-oriented ministry in your church. Who should be involved in the decision-making process? Which ministries will be affected? Do you need to gain the support of anyone outside of the official leadership?

Write down the names of those whose support you need:

1. _____   6. _____

2. _____   7. _____

3. _____   8. _____

4. _____   9. _____

5. _____   10. _____

Facilitate a Receptive Atmosphere

Becoming a gift-oriented church implies change. And change implies going from the known to the unknown. Not everyone will be eager to get involved in this process, unless they are convinced that it is absolutely necessary. Therefore, it is essential to ensure receptiveness among the leadership. The following points may help:

1. Demonstrate the necessity of gift-oriented ministry: The word "necessity" implies that there is a need. Is there dissatisfaction in the church? Why does your church need to become more gift-oriented in its ministry? What motivates your church to change? Discuss these issues with your leadership team.

2. Highlight the gap between what is and what could be: What concept of ministry do your church members have? How can the implementation of a balanced, gift-oriented ministry approach help your church better to reflect on these conceptions? What is the leadership's biblical, theological, and practical understanding of the church? Has an NCD church profile revealed a weakness in the area of gift-oriented ministry? What are the conditions that gave rise to those profile results? Does everyone agree about what needs to be changed?

3. Encourage people to expect positive results: Expectations should be positive, but realistic. Communicate clearly what can be expected as a result of working through a process such as the one found in the *NCD Implementation Resources* for *The 3 Colors of Ministry* in your church.

Reflect upon your own expectations as well. What do you expect personally? (your hopes, your fears)

4. Listen attentively: Pay attention to how your leadership team responds, especially those who are not fully convinced. Listen carefully to their objections and arguments so that you know what to expect from the beginning. Are they afraid of change? Do they reflect preconceived notions? Seek first to understand everyone else's point of view before expecting them to understand yours. If you listen carefully, you will avoid many unnecessary problems.

> *Expectations should be positive, but realistic. Communicate clearly what can be expected as a result of working through this process.*

5. Involve your leaders in the decision-making process: Some churches take for granted that the leadership team will make decisions together. They assume that this is the purpose of a leadership team. Unfortunately, in reality, even churches that have official leadership meetings, not everyone is involved in the decision-making process. Sometimes one leader takes action without consulting the others and the remaining leaders only speak up when they are discontent. This often causes interpersonal conflict and great long-term damage to the church.

If everyone on the leadership team is involved in the planning process, you can expect greater support. People who take part in making a decision are usually more committed to carrying it out than those who are only allowed to stand by and watch while decisions are made without their consent.

Note: At some point in this process, you, along with your leadership team, will need to decide what your personal role in the implementation process will be, and what tasks you will delegate to others.

6. Focus on the "opinion-makers": "Opinion-makers" are the people, who may or may not hold official leadership positions, that influence others to support or to oppose something. They will either facilitate the process or interfere severely. If you have their support, they can contribute greatly to gaining the support of a large enough group of people ("critical mass") to start the process of becoming a truly gift-oriented church.

People who take part in making a decision are usually more committed to carrying it out than those who can only stand by and watch while decisions are made without their consent.

Build good relationships with both kinds of opinion-makers. Listen to them and learn from them. If the ones who slow things down feel like you are taking them seriously and not ignoring them, their opposition might gradually decline.

Make sure that the ones who are pushing things forward are not overdoing it and scaring people away with their energy and enthusiasm. Encourage them to use their relationships and influence wisely.

7. Seek the input of a church consultant: The *NCD Implementation Resources* for *The 3 Colors of Ministry* might open up new horizons for your church. Though it is definitely worthwhile, it can also be a complex process.

If possible, seek the advice and input of someone outside your church who can serve as a consultant throughout the entire process. Talk regularly with this person to evaluate how things are going. The following questions may be helpful: What steps are you preparing for? What has gone well so far? What has not worked? What problems are you facing?

Share the Experience

One of the best ways to gain the support of your leadership team is to encourage them to apply the teaching of *The 3 Colors of Ministry* to their personal lives. You can begin by taking the leadership through the book as you would a small group.

By applying the teaching of *The 3 Colors of Ministry* to your own lives before introducing it to the entire congregation, you allow yourselves to gain experience with the book so that you can interact with the material and evaluate it before sharing it with the rest of the congregation.

The following points will help your leadership team get started:

1. Follow the guidelines for small groups: *How to Study The 3 Colors of Ministry in Your Small Group* has been developed for group leaders to help small group members learn more about spiritual gifts, understand the basics of the three-color approach, identify their own gifts, and apply them in meaningful ministry. Use this tool, designed for small groups, with your leadership team. It includes meeting guidelines, discussion exercises, and suggested "homework."

2. **Structure your meetings:** It is ideal to meet once a week for twelve weeks. Focus your discussions on *The 3 Colors of Ministry*. Do not get side-tracked by other church related issues.

There are different ways to work through these lessons as a leadership team. Choose the way that best fits your situation. Here are some possibilities:

- Include this study as a part of your regular leadership meetings. The disadvantage of this option is that it may overload your meetings and cause you to neglect other important tasks.

- In addition to your regular leadership meetings, schedule weekly or bi-weekly meetings for a set period of time. You might consider reducing the length of your leadership meetings during this period of time in order not to overwhelm anyone.

- Work through the essential material as a weekend course. In many churches, this is the most realistic option because it compresses the preparation phase before implementation. However, this does not yield the same results as a course spread out over several weeks. There is not enough time for the material to thoroughly sink in and be owned by the individual participants.

By applying the teaching of The 3 Colors of Ministry to your own lives before introducing it to the entire congregation, you allow yourselves the chance to interact with the material in advance.

3. **Cover the essential lessons:** Certain lessons must be worked through in order to fully understand the basic principles taught in *The 3 Colors of Ministry*. If you are not able to study all twelve lessons as a leadership team, you should at least go through the following lessons:

Session 1: "The Change Compass"

Session 2: "What is Your Personal Starting Point?"

Session 3: "The Three-Color Gift Test"

Session 10: "The Corporate Starting Point of Your Group"

Session 11: "The Corporate Gifting of your Group"

Session 12: "Let's Celebrate"

4. **Special emphases:** Since the goal of working through *The 3 Colors of Ministry* with a leadership team is different from that of a regular small group, there are a couple of additional emphases that should be made.

List the spiritual gifts that your congregation agrees upon

When working through Chapter 5 of *The 3 Colors of Ministry* (30 spiritual gifts—backgrounds, definitions, practical tips), you as church leaders need to discuss what spiritual gifts are relevant for your church, according to your theological convictions. Make a list of those gifts, with supporting scriptural references (also found in Chapter 5). It does not matter how long your list is. This is important so as to prevent conflicts that might arise if a gift does not fit your theological stance.

You also need to consider how to handle a situation in which someone discovers, according to the *Three-Color Gift Test*, that he or she has one of the "rejected" gifts. Would you be open to having your own theological notions challenged?

Form a team of leaders whose spiritual gifts complement each other

Evaluate thoroughly whether the ministries of each leader correspond with his or her spiritual gifts. What needs to be changed? Is there someone who would find great relief in changing ministry responsibilities, because he has been suffering in the one he has? What ministries have been confirmed by the identification of the corresponding spiritual gifts? Pay attention to feelings of possessiveness and control that may keep people in positions that may not be in accordance with their gifting. It is very important to recognize that God's calling is linked to the spiritual gifts he has given to each individual.

You might consider making a list of all of the leadership team's responsibilities. Consider which gifts are needed for each one. List them according to the best gift scenario, the second-best scenario and an acceptable scenario. Create ministry descriptions for each of those responsibilities and discuss possible changes of responsibilities within your team. If there are ministries for which no one is gifted, consider whether additional people need to be appointed to the team to carry them out. Discuss if there is anyone who should move to another ministry rather than remain on the leadership team.

Don't sacrifice implementation on the church level by forcing premature change within the leadership.

Handle this discussion with great care and sensitivity as it personally affects all leaders at the core of who they are and what they do. However, churches that take this seriously and implement their discoveries will experience a fruitful change. The ministry of the church will flourish as the various ministries are led by people gifted for those tasks. The leadership will experience freedom and renewed motivation, and the pastor will eventually have a team that functions well.

In all of this, it is important to remember that the goal of this process is to implement balanced, gift-oriented ministry within the entire congregation. At this point, if there is opposition among the leaders to this kind of redistribution of assignments, it will suffice to make the leaders aware of this possibility. Don't sacrifice implementation on the church level by forcing premature change within the leadership.

Step 2:
Find a Ministry Coordinator

Having the *vision* for implementing balanced, gift-oriented ministry in your church does not necessarily imply becoming the *specialist* to carry it out. Find the appropriately gifted and interested person who can focus his or her attention on initiating and integrating this process into the life of the church. This is not to say that you may not be the right person for this job. However, if you are the pastor of your church, most likely you are already a very busy person. Taking on more than you can handle portrays the exact opposite of what a gift-oriented approach is all about. Maybe another member of your leadership team, or another person in your church, has the necessary spiritual gifts to carry out this responsibility. If this person already holds a leadership position within the church, he or she must be able to give up some current leadership responsibilities in order to take over this important task.

> *Having the vision for implementing balanced, gift-oriented ministry in your church does not necessarily imply becoming the specialist to carry it out.*

The Necessary Gifts

The gift mix of the person in charge of this implementation process should include one or more of the following:

1. The gift of leadership. This person will be forming and leading a team of volunteers.

2. The gift of organization. This person needs to be able to create a structure that will successfully relate gifted church members to the various ministry opportunities available within the church.

3. The gift of teaching. This person will be training and equipping gift counselors and seminar leaders.

It is not essential for a candidate to have all three of these gifts. It is also not important that they be equally developed. However, if the Ministry Coordinator does not have all three gifts, it is important that he or she work in a team that will complement his or her gift mix.

Develop a Ministry Description

Before you begin your search for the coordinator of this implementation process, develop a ministry description for this position, with the help of your leadership team. Use Worksheet E (page 64) and the "Ministry Coordinator Ministry Description" sample offered on page 27 as a guide.

The time that this coordinator will put into this task each week is hard to calculate exactly. However, in order to get started, he or she will need to invest at least five to seven hours a week. The more time he or she puts in, the sooner progress will be made.

The coordinator should not quit before the conclusion of the start-up phase. In other words, a team of counselors needs to be in place, some seminars or small group experiences need to have taken place, and the whole process needs to be functioning before any changes are made in the leadership of this task. For this reason, it is difficult to define the duration of the coordinator's ministry. Nevertheless, at the conclusion of the start-up phase, it is good to consider whether the present coordinator continues to be the right person for the responsibility.

Search for Suitable Candidates

Consider who would be good candidates for coordinating implementation in your church. Do they belong to the church leadership team? What are their spiritual gifts? Do these people already serve in the church? Is there anyone who is already familiar with the gift-oriented approach, has discovered his or her gifts, and has the right gift mix for the task? You may wish to ask your leadership team whom they believe would be good candidates.

At the conclusion of the start-up phase it is good to consider whether the present coordinator continues to be the right person for the responsibility.

Make a list of at least three potential candidates, including those who may not meet all of the criteria perfectly. What are the factors in favor of each candidate? What are the factors against them? Rank them according to your order of preference. Meet with them in this order and explain the concept to them, casting your vision so that they fully understand what this responsibility entails and can decide whether or not they should take this ministry upon themselves.

The following pages are directed predominantly to the coordinator. They include all the necessary information and instructions for implementing balanced, gift-oriented ministry in your church. To effectively prepare your newly-selected coordinator, discuss all of the critical issues with him or her and then give him or her this manual. This person should have a contact person within the leadership team (if he or she is not a member of the church leadership) who can lend his or her support when needed and can help evaluate the progress of the implementation process.

If you cannot find suitable candidates, move on to the next step of encouraging the volunteers and leaders of your church to go through *The 3 Colors of Ministry* in a small group format. While going through this process, you can search for appropriate candidates.

In some cases, it may be necessary for the pastor or a member of the church leadership team to carry out this start-up phase. However, because this is a large, time-consuming task, once the start-up is completed, this responsibility should probably be delegated to another person.

Ministry Coordinator
Ministry Description

Task	Date
Ministry Coordinator	March 1, 2001

Goals
To coordinate the implementation of balanced, gift-oriented ministry in the church.

Sub-tasks
(1) Gain the support of the leaders   (2) Form an implementation team   (3) Create and maintain a list of all church-related ministries   (4) Develop ministry descriptions and keep them up-to-date (5) Initiate seminars, small group processes, and gift counseling

Contact people
Responsible for: Gift counselors, gift seminar leaders, and ministry assistants
Responsible to: Senior pastor and elder board
Work with: Small group leaders, gift counselors, seminar leaders, and ministry assistants

Spiritual gifts	Abilities/Interests
Leadership	Understand the gift-oriented approach and NCD.
Teaching	Be able to master complex tasks and processes.
Organization	Work well with a team.
	Have a pioneering spirit.

Time commitment	Length of assignment
5 to 7 hours a week	Initially, until end of start-up phase. Two years?

Training
Read: *The 3 Colors of Ministry, How to Implement the 3 Colors of Ministry in Your Church,* and *How to Use the 3 Colors of Ministry in a Mentoring Relationship*

Additional agreements
Quarterly update the elder board on progress of implementation.

Step 3: Introduce Your Other Leaders to the Process

As was previously mentioned, vision is an important ingredient in motivating your church to become gift-oriented. At this point, the church leadership team has gone through the implementation process. Now is the time to let the ministry and small group leaders catch a vision for the implementation of balanced, gift-oriented ministry in the church. Not only is this the next, most natural step in multiplying this ministry, but it is also the step in which you will discover potential candidates for the counseling team that will be formed later on. In principle, this step is the same as Step 1, in which the leadership team studied *The 3 Colors of Ministry*. Begin by considering who should be involved in this process and how to introduce them to it.

Who Are the Leaders?

Make a list of all of the volunteers who hold key positions in your church. This could include small group leaders, the children's and youth ministries' staff, the worship service leaders and the leaders of the counseling ministry. They should be volunteers who oversee an entire area of ministry and are responsible for other volunteers. Once again, you want to ask whose support you need to gain in order to implement this approach to ministry in the entire church. These are the people who will multiply the process later on, so be sure to involve as many of them as possible at this point.

How do You Want to Introduce the Material?

At this point you need to decide if these leaders will go through a small group process or a seminar, what material needs to be discussed, and what the schedule will be. Since experience reveals that it is more difficult to get volunteers from different ministries together for a small group process than it is to get the leadership team together, a seminar format may be a good option for this group of people. Someone who has the gift of teaching and has been a part of the process so far, maybe even the pastor, should prepare to teach this seminar.

Now it is time to let the ministry and small group leaders catch a vision for the implementation of balanced, gift-oriented ministry in the church.

What You should Take into Account

Personally invite the small group and ministry leaders to the training event (or process) you have planned and scheduled. A personal invitation by the pastor will convey the importance of this training to each volunteer, especially those who have reservations or do not fully understand what this is all about. Since it is important that everyone participate, you may want to offer an alternative date for those who would not be able to participate otherwise.

Through this training process, your leaders will identify or confirm their spiritual gifts and determine where to apply them. Cover the topics of at least the six most essential sessions found in *How to Study The 3 Colors of Ministry in Your Small Group* (see page 23).

Facilitate the Sharing of Personal Experiences

Once your ministry and small group leaders have confirmed their spiritual gifts in a small group or a seminar, they should go through a counseling session. However, since there are no gift counselors available yet, it is imperative to facilitate the sharing of personal experiences among the participants. At the end of the process, divide the participants into groups of three, making sure that they know each other well, and have them discuss the following questions:

Since there are no gift counselors available yet, it is imperative to facilitate the sharing of personal experiences among the participants.

- What spiritual gifts do you believe the other two individuals in your group have?
- What were your *Three-Color Gift Test* results?
- Do your test results and the assessment of others agree? In what ways?
- What are your current ministry involvements?
- Do your spiritual gifts correspond to your ministries?
- Is there anything that needs to be changed? If yes, what?
- What were your *Change Compass* results?
- How do you believe you could best grow in the use of your gifts?
- Do you see value in the use of *The 3 Colors of Ministry* in your ministry area? What would you expect to see happen as a result of studying it and applying it consistently?

Step 4: Form a Gift-Oriented Ministry Implementation Team

G ift-oriented ministry implies saying goodbye to the "superman" servant who does everything all by himself or herself. It is essential for the body of Christ that the different gifts complement each other in each area of ministry. This also applies to the ministry of implementing this approach in your church.

The goal of this process is to transform the entire congregation into a gift-oriented church.

While it is the Ministry Coordinator's task to initiate and coordinate the implementation process, he or she will need help in at least three different areas: gift-counseling, teaching seminars, and administering the implementation process. Gather a team of volunteers whose spiritual gifts complement one another, to work with you in these areas and to share your vision for a balanced, gift-oriented church. This does not mean that you cannot be involved in these areas as well if you have the necessary spiritual gifts. Yet, without a team, you will not be able to cope with all of the demands of the entire ministry.

Proceed Gradually

By this time, all of the small group and ministry leaders in your church have taken the *Three-Color Gift Test*. Search for those individuals who could potentially join your implementation team. Make sure they have the appropriate gifts, and are able to take on additional tasks or turn over former ministry involvements, if necessary.

The goal of this process is to transform the entire congregation into a gift-oriented church. This process will take place over an extended period of time and will not turn the church around overnight. If you cannot find enough members for your team initially, start with those you have. As individuals discover their gifts, you will discover more volunteers to take over different aspects of your training and organizational responsibilities.

Find and Train Gift Counselors

It is the task of the gift counselor to help individual Christians, who have discovered their spiritual gifts, find a suitable place of ministry in the church and exercise their gifts in an effective manner. This is done in their counseling sessions with individuals as they discuss together the results of the tests in *The 3 Colors of Ministry*, the counselee's interests, abilities, availability, and the ministry possibilities available within the church. The gift counselor helps create a bridge between the individual's gifts and specific ministry tasks by putting him or her in contact with the right people and ministries.

When looking for gift counselors, keep in mind the need for the following gifts: wisdom, organization, counseling, discernment, and teaching. The gift of wisdom is beneficial for advising others and applying theoretical knowledge to concrete situations. The gift of organization is helpful for keeping track of the various ministry opportunities in the entire church and for effectively carrying out the individual consultations. Christians gifted in counseling are good listeners, an important aspect of gift counseling. The gift of discernment is useful for identifying when someone has not properly assessed himself or herself through the *Three-Color Gift Test* or when someone is on the wrong track with what they believe their calling is. The gift of teaching can be a benefit in gift counseling when it is discovered that basic truths have been misunderstood, despite having attended gift seminars or studied a book. Of course, gift counselors do not need to have all of these gifts, however, one or two should be found in their gift mix.

Develop a ministry description for gift counselors. The example on page 33 may be helpful in this process.

How to Train Gift Counselors

Gift Counselors can be trained in at least three ways: (1) by studying the Mentor's Guide, (2) by participating in an interactive training seminar, and (3) by means of on-the-job training

1. Mentor's Guide: Give every gift counselor a copy of the booklet *How to Use The 3 Colors of Ministry in a Mentoring Relationship*. It is basically a gift-counselor's manual. Ask them to work through it completely. In so doing, they will gain all the knowledge necessary to carry out a gift-counseling appointment.

2. Interactive training seminar: The gift counselor's task is crucial to the success of this implementation process. Therefore, he or she should not only know the theory of gift counseling, but should also have experience in applying that theory to real situations.

Once you have found several potential gift counselors, meet with them to review *How to Use The 3 Colors of Ministry in a Mentoring Relationship*, answer their questions, and learn by role play how to conduct appointments. This training course does not have to be long. You may want to offer it for part of a day or on one or more evenings.

The gift counselor helps create a bridge between the individual's gifts and specific ministry tasks by putting him or her in contact with the right people and ministries.

Cast the Vision: One of the training seminar's goals is to cast your vision for the implementation of the gift-oriented approach to ministry throughout the church. Thoroughly think through how you can communicate to the seminar participants the importance of the gift counselor's task. Show them how their ministry relates to the entire implementation process. Share your expectations for the church as a result of this implementation process. Answer the following questions: What does the church look like right now? What will the church look like in the future as a result of gift counseling? What positive changes do you expect to see in the church? Using word pictures (like the story of the animal school on page 8 of the Mentor's Guide) to help convey your vision and inspire the gift counselors for their task, can be very effective.

Train: Work through *How to Use the 3 Colors of Ministry in a Mentoring Relationship* on your own, highlighting the details that you want to point out or emphasize in your training course. As you read, ask yourself the following questions: What is so important for prospective gift counselors to know that they should not only read it but hear it? What points would I like to embellish? What would I suggest they do differently?

Keep in mind that the emphasis of the gift counselor training course is learning by doing.

You might want to present these things to them formally, but keep in mind that the emphasis of this training course is to learn by doing.

Discuss: Your presentation should be followed by a question and answer time. Allow enough time for this. Make sure your gift counselors know that you are their contact person should any questions arise in the future. If you have developed a ministry organization chart, give them a copy so that they can see the big picture of who is involved and what their respective responsibilities are. (Worksheet B: "Structuring Your Implementation Team" might serve as a reference.)

Practice: Use the following structure for giving your counselors-in-training a "hands-on" experience:

1. Model the first phase of a session with a volunteer. Inform the volunteer ahead of time so that he or she will have his or her *Change Compass* and *Three-Color Gift Test* results in hand.

2. Following your role play, give the prospective counselors an opportunity to discuss what they have observed, both positive and negative (experienced counselors are not perfect either!).

3. Divide the prospective counselors into groups of three. One person in each group will take on the role of counselor; another, the role of counselee; and the third will observe the other two as they role play part of a counseling session. Have them practice the same phase that they have just observed. They will use the real test results of the person playing the part of the counselee. Conclude this exercise by sharing observations and changing roles. In all, this role play will be done three times.

Once these three exercises are completed using the first phase of a counseling session, repeat them with the next phase. Continue in this way until all of the counseling session phases have been covered.

Allow four to five hours to complete this "hands-on" training. Intersperse breaks between each series of exercises, as this training can be

Gift Counselor
Ministry Description

Task	Date
Gift Counselor	March 1, 2001

Goals
To advise members in such a way that (a) their spiritual gifts are confirmed, (b) they find their most suitable place of ministry, and (c) they are challenged to mature in the skillful use of their gifts.

Sub-tasks
(1) To stay informed about current ministry opportunities   (2) To schedule gift counseling sessions
(3) To counsel   (4) To follow up   (5) To forward information to the Ministry Coordinator

Contact people
Responsible for: Church members who need guidance in spiritual gifts and ministry involvements
Responsible to: Ministry Coordinator
Work with: Small group leaders and seminar leaders

Spiritual gifts	Abilities/Interests
At least one or two of these gifts:	Understand the gift-oriented approach.
wisdom, organization, counseling,	Interact well with people.
discernment, teaching	Listen attentively.
	Lead discussions.

Time commitment	Length of assignment
Approximately one to two hour per interview	One year, renewable

Training
Read: *The 3 Colors of Ministry* and
How to Use the 3 Colors of Ministry in a Mentoring Relationship

Additional agreements

quite intense. Make sure that every participant has enough copies of the "Discussion Outline" (Worksheet 1 in the Mentor's Guide) to be able to take notes as they go.

Conclusion: At the end of the training course, have the participants divide into groups of three to review what they have learned. Ask the following questions: What did you learn that was new to you? What unanswered questions do you still have? In what areas do you need to do further study? Conclude with a brief time of sharing as a large group.

> *The members of your church will most likely identify their gifts in the context of a small group or a seminar.*

3. On-the-job training: It is good to offer prospective gift counselors the opportunity to learn from experienced gift counselors by watching them at work in a counseling appointment. Few opportunities are as effective as this for learning how to do gift counseling.

Make sure to inform "new" gift counselors about scheduled counseling appointments so that they can take advantage of those opportunities to observe and learn. It is helpful for the counselor and the counselor-in-training to meet before the appointment in order to run over the counselor's plan. Introduce the counselee to the counselor-in-training, explaining that he or she is there to observe the session as a part of his or her gift-counselor training. The counselor-in-training should not step into the conversation at any point. He or she is there to observe only. Following the appointment, evaluate the session together. Ask the following questions: What are your observations? What did you learn? Did the session proceed as expected? What problems arose?

Later in the training process, the counselor and counselor-in-training can change roles so that the experienced counselor has the opportunity to observe and give feedback to the less experienced counselor.

Find and Train Seminar Leaders

The members of your church will most likely identify their gifts in the context of a small group or a seminar. For the small group setting, the book *How to Study The 3 Colors of Ministry in Your Small Group* is a simple guide to help leaders take their groups through *The 3 Colors of Ministry* without any special training. The only thing the coordinator needs to do is encourage them to get involved in the implementation process and hand them the book.

However, not all church members are involved in a small group or are ready to get involved in this implementation process from the outset. Therefore, it is helpful to offer gift seminars on a regular basis.

In order to offer such seminars, it is necessary to have qualified seminar leaders: individuals who have the gift of teaching and can prepare and carry out a seminar based on *The 3 Colors of Ministry*. A seminar leader's preparation and presentation can be greatly enhanced by taking advantage of the graphics available on the CD-ROM that is included with this book.

In many churches one seminar leader will suffice. In larger churches, more than one seminar leader may be needed. The ministry description on the next page will give you an idea of what this responsibility could look like in your church.

Find and Train Assistants

While it is very helpful to have a gift counselor and a seminar leader from the outset, it may not be necessary to have additional assistance for this implementation process in the beginning. Depending on the size of your church, where your church is in the process, and the amount of work that you personally can handle, it may be necessary to delegate some of your administrative tasks. You, as the coordinator, need to be continually thinking about what tasks you can delegate and to whom. Individuals who have the gift of helps are great candidates. It is a joy for them to be able to support you, relieve some of your stress, and use their gifts to complement yours. For example, you may wish to delegate the task of maintaining lists, files, or the database of ministry opportunities, ministry descriptions, and the church member's gifts.

Search for a Co-leader

At some point in the process, you should look for a co-leader. A co-leader is someone who will gradually be enabled to take over your ministry position. Why is a co-leader important? A co-leader can relieve you of some of your ministry responsibilities. He or she can represent you when you are on vacation or unable to attend to your responsibilities for any other reason. He or she could take over should you feel led to move on to another ministry. He or she can also play an important role if the ministry is expanding and multiplying.

Depending on the size of your church, where your church is in the process, and the amount of work that you personally can handle, it may be necessary to delegate some of your administrative tasks.

Your co-leader should have the appropriate spiritual gifts, even if they are in the latent gift category. When you first begin to work together, allow this person to watch you at work. Then, involve him or her little by little in your work by assigning limited responsibilities until he or she has performed each one under your supervision at least once in the course of a year. When you notice that your co-leader is able to work on his or her own, this person can either take over your role or continue to work with you unsupervised. However, you should continue to be his or her ministry contact person.

**Chapter 2:
Getting Started**

Gift Seminar Leader
Ministry Description

Task	Date
Gift Seminar Leader	March 1, 2001

Goals
To conduct seminars as a means of helping members of the church discover their spiritual gifts.

Sub-tasks
(1) To prepare a seminar based on *The 3 Colors of Ministry*
(2) To conduct the seminar on a regular basis in the church
(3) To encourage seminar attendees to set up an appointment with a gift counselor

Contact people
Responsible for: Church members who want to identify their spiritual gifts
Responsible to: Ministry Coordinator
Work with: Gift Counselors

Spiritual gifts	Abilities/Interests
Teaching	Understand and promote the gift-oriented approach.
	Moderate large group discussions well.

Time commitment	Length of assignment
Depends on seminar format and frequency	One year, renewable

Training
Read: *The 3 Colors of Ministry* and
How to Study the 3 Colors of Ministry in a Small Group

Additional agreements
Ministry Coordinator has graphics from which color overhead transparencies can be made.

Step 5: Define All Ministry Positions and Ministry Descriptions

The following steps in the implementation process presuppose that a complete overview of the ministry positions in the church has been developed. Included in this overview are those tasks that do not exist, but are wanted. New ministries may also need to be developed when it is discovered that there are people whose gifts and interests may not fit into the mold of previously existing ministries. Remember that the goal of gift counseling is not just to fill job openings. Rather, it is to find ministries that are suited to the God-given uniqueness of each individual. Taking this into consideration ahead of time helps focus church activities.

Usually there is no one who has a comprehensive view of all the various ministries in the church.

Work in a Team

Usually there is no one who has a comprehensive view of all the various ministries in the church. Nor is there anyone who has all potential ministries in mind. Potential ministries are usually recognized "on the spot," when a need reveals a deficit.

Therefore, when you create your ministry list, include the church leaders, gift counselors, and volunteer leaders in the process. You might want to get together to discuss all areas of ministry. Or, you might ask each one to submit a list of all the ministries under their supervision, as well as those tasks that go beyond their current sphere of responsibility but might be added in the future.

By including gift counselors in this process, you will be giving them the opportunity to have a better grasp of the ministry positions available in the church. Since it is their task to suggest ministry opportunities to their counselees, they need to be well-informed.

Diagram all Church Ministries

It may be helpful to represent existing ministries in the form of a diagram. Include the large areas of ministry, for example, Children's Ministry, Youth Ministry, Small Group Ministry, Worship Team, Gift-Oriented Ministry Implementation Team, etc. Then ask: What are the individual tasks that make up each of these areas of ministry? What ministry positions and tasks have been filled? By whom? Are there any other structures or sub-structures in place? If yes, what do they look like? Be careful not to overlook any tasks that are not clearly integrated into the structure of the ministry, nor any tasks that are not "officially" recognized, such as intercessors or small group hosts.

Write a Ministry Description for Every Single Responsibility

This task should also be carried out together with your leaders and gift counselors. Together you will decide on the details of each ministry mentioned in the ministry list you have just made, i.e., goals, tasks, spiritual gifts, interests, and abilities necessary to complete that job. These ministry descriptions will help you know for whom to look when filling each ministry. They are also a helpful reference tool for those who volunteer for a task. It enables them to see exactly what is expected of them, how much time they will need to invest and what preparation they need.

Ministry descriptions will help you know for whom to look when filling each ministry. They are also a helpful reference tool for those who volunteer for a task. It enables them to see exactly what is expected of them.

1. Name the task or ministry: Under "Task," write the name of the task or ministry under consideration.

2. Fill in the date: Include the date on which you drew up this version of the ministry description. Ministry responsibilities may change, so it is helpful to know when each ministry description was made. If you give the worksheet to a new volunteer, enter the date he or she received the ministry description and took on this assignment.

3. Set goals: What is to be accomplished by the respective task or ministry? State these goals in measurable and concise terms.

4. Outline the most important details of the task: As illustrated in the ministry description for the coordinator of the implementation process, the gift counselors, and the seminar leaders, every task or ministry contains a number of sub-tasks. Take your time as you develop each ministry description. Discuss the following questions together: What does this task cover in detail? What does it take to prepare and train individuals for this task or ministry? How should this task be carried out? What needs to be done in order to keep this task or ministry up-to-date? Does this assignment involve administration, follow-up, or cooperation with other individuals?

It is not necessary to include every little detail of the job under "Subtasks." Rather, seek to summarize all of these details into four or five main categories.

5. Determine for whom and to whom this person is responsible: There are three things to be considered: (1) If applicable, for whom does this volunteer assume responsibility? (2) To whom does this person report? In other words, who is his or her contact person or supervisor? (3) With whom does this person work? With whom does he or she need to keep up-to-date, coordinate his or her work, and stay in touch?

6. List the spiritual gifts that are needed: How do you discover what spiritual gifts are needed for a specific assignment? At the end of this book you will find a questionnaire (Worksheet D) that will help you decide what spiritual gifts correspond to each task. In addition, we have included a list of common ministries with their corresponding gifts (Appendix A).

7. Record the necessary abilities and interests: Though spiritual gifts are key to finding one's place in ministry, they are not the only criterion. As you know, the same spiritual gift can be used in different ways. Someone who has the gift of teaching can use this gift in a children's Sunday School class, in an adult class, in a small group discussion, or in front of a large audience. A person who has the gift of evangelism may feel more comfortable sharing Christ in one-on-one conversations with his or her neighbors than proclaiming the good news on a busy street corner. Another Christian may not be able to see himself or herself in any other role than proclaiming Christ in front of a large audience.

These examples illustrate that people may have the same spiritual gifts, but very different preferences. Because our interests, abilities, passions, and personalities differ, we cannot simply assign spiritual gifts to tasks without taking into consideration the differences in people who have those gifts. For this reason it is important to include the necessary inclinations and interests in each ministry description.

To help you think through these different interests and inclinations, consider the following:

- different age-groups (children, youth, adults, senior citizens)
- different social groups (singles, students, handicapped persons, refugees, and so on)
- different issues related to the church or community (politics, third-world needs, abortion, church planting, discipleship, etc.)

After thinking through the necessary spiritual gifts and interests, focus your thoughts on the abilities that are a result of one's personality, education, and/or training. Thinking of one's professional competence might be of great help when you are looking for a janitor, librarian, bookkeeper, etc.

Aside from professional skills, you should consider those skills that people acquire throughout the course of life. For example, if a specific ministry requires motivational skills, look for someone who has those skills. Do you need someone who can think analytically, has good people skills, or can communicate well? If so, include those things in the ministry description.

Though spiritual gifts are key to finding one's place in ministry, they are not the only criterion.

8. Determine how much time needs to be invested: Think about how much time a volunteer will need to invest on a daily, weekly, or monthly basis in preparation, training, and carrying out each ministry.

Try to be realistic. If your expectations are too high, you will turn off potential volunteers. If your expectations are too low, volunteers may drop out of their ministry before their term of service has expired. If you find it difficult to recruit a volunteer for a time-consuming task or ministry, consider how you could change the task in order to minimize the time requirement. You might also consider dividing it up into two separate ministry descriptions.

9. Define the length of the assignment: Do not assign tasks for a lifetime. It often makes sense to assign a task for one year. Following this time period, evaluate your volunteer's ministry involvement together and give him or her the option of ending or extending his or her involvement for another year.

10. Consider the type of training that will be offered: Just because someone has the appropriate spiritual gifts and abilities does not guarantee a successful start in ministry or a good participation long term. Training and supervision are often necessary. Define how volunteers will be trained for each ministry. This might include anything from a two-minute introduction, to a two-hour presentation, to specialized training over the course of several weeks.

Extending the Implementation Process

The previous chapter focused on preparation and implementation at the level of church leadership. This chapter focuses on the congregation as a whole, and is designed to help you take a balanced, gift-oriented approach to ministry all the way down to the newest member of your congregation. It also provides some thoughts on fine tuning your implementation as you go along. Remember, your congregation is unique, and at some point in the process there should be thoughtful customization of ongoing, long-term implementation.

Step 6: Initiate Seminars, Small Groups, and Counseling

Congratulations! Having arrived at this point signifies that you have done all of the necessary preparatory steps. Now the entire church can get involved in this implementation process. The gift-oriented approach to ministry will now be made public, and everyone in the church will have the opportunity to discover his or her spiritual gifts and put them into practice.

The gift-oriented approach to ministry will now be made public, and everyone in the church will have the opportunity to discover his or her spiritual gifts and put them into practice.

To be sure, the *intention* is that the entire church get involved, yet the extent of individual participation must be up to the individual. Nobody should be pressured to take part in a seminar, small group, gift-counseling session, etc. Rather, allow the enthusiasm of those who have discovered and applied their spiritual gifts to naturally motivate other individuals to get involved.

The fact that this process is voluntary has two consequences: (1) It will take time for the ministries of the entire church to become gift-oriented; and (2) different "tracks" for gift discovery need to be offered. In this step we suggest three different tracks you could try in combination with each other. They include gift seminars, small group studies, and gift counseling.

Offer Spiritual Gifts Seminars

Before you can offer spiritual-gift-discovery seminars, you must have a seminar leader. The seminar leader should develop his or her own seminar based on *The 3 Colors of Ministry*.

New church members. The simplest way to introduce a new program is by offering it to those for whom every program is new. The best time to invite people to a spiritual-gift-discovery seminar is when they first join your church, either because they recently moved to the area or because they have just come to faith in Christ.

At this point, start a new program and invite all new members to a "Gift-Oriented Living" seminar. In some churches, participation in this kind of seminar will be completely voluntary. In other churches, it can be easily included as one of the membership requirements (membership class, baptism class, etc.). Usually new church members appreciate this kind of opportunity since they are eager to get to know people and to learn more about the ministry options in the church.

Established church members. The other target group are those people who have been members of the church for many years. They, too, should be given the opportunity to discover their spiritual gifts in a seminar format.

Schedule "Gift-Oriented Living" seminars on a regular basis and invite established members to attend. In order to reach as many members as possible, it is good to vary the seminar format. Offer it as a weekend seminar, a seminar spread out over several consecutive evenings, and as once-a-week sessions for a number of weeks.

You may also want to invite established members to join a seminar for new members. In one church, every prospective member is required to attend a New Member's Class that meets on Wednesday night for four weeks. The first two meetings are about church-related issues: What is the church's vision? How is the church organized? What are the church's theological convictions? Meetings three and four are focused on discovering one's spiritual gifts and each new member is given the opportunity to sign up for a gift-counseling session. These four meetings are always open to all church members, giving everyone at least two or three additional opportunities each year to participate in a spiritual gift-discovery seminar.

Start Small Group Studies

Many of your small group leaders have already discovered their spiritual gifts and have learned to apply them in Step 3. They have begun to experience for themselves the joy of living and serving according to their own personal gifting. These small group leaders are your connection to a large portion of your church body—the members of their small groups. As leaders, they know the members personally, understand their strengths and weaknesses, and perhaps have even helped them identify one or more spiritual gifts. It is natural for these small group leaders to be the ones to help their group members discover and find a place to use their spiritual gifts. In fact, this essential task should be included in their ministry descriptions!

In order to reach as many members as possible, it is good to vary the seminar format. Offer weekend seminars, seminars spread out over several consecutive evenings, and six once-a-week seminars.

Therefore, contact your small group leaders on a regular basis. Encourage them to offer a series of studies on spiritual gifts using the book, *How to Study The 3 Colors of Ministry in Your Small Group*. Make it your goal for all small groups to work through *The 3 Colors of Ministry*. Depending on the character of a group, it might be worth encouraging the leaders to repeat this process from time to time. (Please note that this may not be a meaningful exercise for every group!)

Aside from the small groups that already exist, you might want to start some "gift-discovery groups" that meet for a limited period of time. These groups would focus their studies exclusively on spiritual gifts. There are various ways to do this: Small group leaders and even entire small groups might choose to serve the congregation in a special way, for a limited period of time, by opening up to other church members as "gift-discovery groups." Also, volunteers who usually offer gift-discovery seminars may also want to offer weekly evening meetings to help people discover and learn how to use their spiritual gifts in an informal, small group context. This kind of informality does not happen, of course, in the lecture style of a seminar, but rather in a discussion format as suggested in *How to Study The 3 Colors of Ministry in Your Small Group*.

If it is difficult for your church to motivate small group leaders to get involved in a new project, pay attention to the following three things:

1. It is very important for your small group leaders to experience *The 3 Colors of Ministry* in a small group format and then to be able to serve in the church according to their spiritual gifts. If they are not inspired as individuals, they will not inspire others. If they are not serving according to their spiritual gifting, they will find it hard to assist others in finding gift-oriented ministries.

2. Do not overload your small group leaders. They have limited time and energy just like anyone else. So, since the small group process is essential to the success of becoming a gift-oriented church, you may want to consider ways to relieve the small group leaders of some of their tasks.

3. Offer training or coaching. Demonstrate a small group study for your group leaders over a period of several weeks, using *How to Study The 3 Colors of Ministry in Your Small Group*. Stress to them that leading their group through this process is quite simple since the lessons have already been prepared. Make yourself available to the small group leaders as they are working through this book in their individual groups. Coach them or make an agreement with the director of small group ministries (if your church has such a position) to coach them throughout this process, in order to make it easier for them.

Aside from the groups that already exist, you might want to start some "gift discovery groups" for a limited period of time.

Offer Gift Counseling

Many Christians can get frustrated before they find a meaningful ministry to be involved in, because they do not know how to proceed once they have discovered their gifts. They come pretty close to reaching the goal of appropriately applying their gifts, but they do not make the transition to meaningfully serving in a church ministry. That is the role of the gift counselors, who have one of the most crucial tasks in the implementation process.

The purpose of gift counseling is to help Christians who have identified their spiritual gifts interpret the test results accurately; recognize their interests, inclinations, and skills; realistically assess their availability; and come to the right conclusions about ministry involvement. It also serves to assist them in thinking about how they need to grow in the application of their gifts. Furthermore, the counselor gives them contact information for potential tasks or ministries and agrees with them on the next steps that need to be taken.

It is very important, then, to include the scheduling of one-on-one gift-counseling appointments as part of the follow-up to a seminar or a small group study. Make an agreement with your gift counselors to be available to do individual counseling with participants in the days immediately following each seminar. And make an agreement with your small group leaders to encourage their small group members to schedule an appointment with a gift counselor. You may even want to suggest that the group leaders invite a gift counselor to one of their meetings to explain this ministry and schedule appointments.

It is very important to include the scheduling of one-on-one gift counseling appointments as part of the follow-up to a seminar or a small group study.

To help keep the gift counselors up-to-date, communicate the following information on a regular basis:

- What tasks and ministry positions are available in the church (updated ministry descriptions)?
- What tasks and ministry positions are currently vacant and need volunteers?
- What new ministry positions could be created if the appropriate volunteers were found?

It is a good idea to write up a summary of available or potential ministry positions on a regular basis. You may want to delegate this task to a volunteer on your team.

Step 7: Do Your Implementation Housekeeping

The implementation process does not end with the seminars, the small group studies, or even the individual appointments. There is still some homework to be done, though not necessarily by the Ministry Coordinator. Nevertheless, the coordinator needs to make sure that *someone* is doing this work.

Make Sure that Follow-up Happens

It is important that the gift counselors follow up to make sure that their counselees have been in touch with the recommended contact persons. They must not take for granted that this contact will happen! Therefore, as the Ministry Coordinator, you need to make sure that two to three weeks after their one-on-one meeting, the gift counselors are making these follow-up calls. *How to Use The 3 Colors of Ministry in a Mentoring Relationship* provides more information regarding the details and organization of these follow-up tasks.

The implementation process does not end with the seminars, the small group studies, or even with the individual appointments.

Maintain the Member and Ministry Databases

Suppose a volunteer in the children's ministry department quits. In order for the ministry to continue, you desperately need to find a new volunteer. How can you quickly replace this individual with someone who has the appropriate spiritual gifts? Are you going to wait for the next gift-discovery seminar to find a qualified person?

In this situation, a database that contains all of the church members and is organized according to their spiritual gifts would be extremely helpful for finding a qualified person. It would be a simple task of looking under the gifts needed to discover who you need to contact.

If you are interested in this kind of a system, set up two databases. The first one should be organized according to all of the tasks in the church and should contain the corresponding ministry descriptions. The other should contain all of the church members and their spiritual gifts.

Once you have this set up, the task of finding ministry personnel is greatly facilitated. In the above scenario, for example, you would first look under "Children's Ministry" in the Ministry database. In the corresponding ministry description you may discover that "shepherd" and "teacher" are the necessary spiritual gifts for this task, and that an interest in spending time with kids is a necessary qualification. At this point, you would look up the spiritual gifts, "shepherd" and "teacher," in the Member database. You may discover that John, Nancy, Amy, and Bill all have these gifts, but that Nancy is the only one who is also interested in working with kids, making Nancy a perfect first choice for filling this ministry vacancy.

As was illustrated above, the Ministry database needs to be organized according to the individual tasks in the church and each one needs to include a detailed ministry description that lists the spiritual gifts, interests, and skills needed, and the amount of time to be invested. The Member database should be organized according to the individual spiritual gifts and should contain the following information: spiritual gift, name, address, phone number, additional gifts (manifest/latent), interests/skills, availability, current ministry involvement, date of gift consultation, and date of data entry or last update.

How many gifts a person has will determine how many times he or she appears in the database. Each person will need to appear in the database under each gift that he or she has. This information is easily discovered by the gift counselors when they meet with individual counselees. Make sure to get updated information from your gift counselors on a regular basis.

Keeping these files up-to-date takes some time. You may want to consider delegating this responsibility to someone who has the spiritual gifts of organization and helps.

Training and Introduction to Ministry

Make sure that new volunteers are trained and receive a good introduction to their ministry. Training options should be included in each ministry description, and ministry leaders should be reminded to introduce new people to their task in a thorough manner.

In one church, a person was in charge of the overhead transparencies for worship. This person's task was to place the appropriate overhead transparency on the overhead projector whenever a new song was to be sung. To do this very simple task, only the universal Christian responsibility of "service" was required. However, the worship team was repeatedly frustrated, since the person doing the task did not know how to use an overhead projector. Had he been given a brief introduction to the use of the projector before he started, this problem would never have occurred.

Keeping these files up-to-date takes some time. You may want to consider delegating this responsibility to someone who has the spiritual gifts of organization and helps.

In addition to giving a thorough introduction and adequate training, it is important for the ministry director to integrate the new volunteer into his or her team. The volunteer needs to feel welcomed and a part of the team. Though this may seem obvious, ministry directors are often unaware of this important part of their job. You, as Ministry Coordinator can help them by drawing their attention to this responsibility.

Step 8: Pursue Greater Balance in Your Church's Ministry Profile

N ow that you have taken a good percentage, perhaps even the majority, of your church members through the process of dis- covering their gifts and getting involved in ministry, you have enough information to do some evaluation. This can be an exciting step for your team as you take a panoramic look at the entire ministry of your church.

Set aside some time as an implementation team to survey where you've been, and more importantly, where you should head in the future.

You have already come a long way in increasing the gift-ori- entation of your church's ministry. Surely by now you are beginning to see some positive changes. People are more fulfilled. Ministries are more effective. A larger percentage of the congregation is involved. Your team should be pleased with these results.

However, some important issues may have surfaced during this time. Have you "out-grown" your existing ministry struc- ture? Have you discovered that there are members with cer- tain gifts and interests, but no appropriate ministries to place them in? Are there any patterns that have become apparent? Are there any neglected areas that require special attention? Questions such as these should stimulate further reflection on the part of your team and the leadership of your church.

Set aside some time as an implementation team to survey where you've been, and more importantly, where you should go in the future. Your specific goal, at this point in the process, should be to create an environment in which gift-oriented ministry can be pursued long-term in your church, and pursued in a truly balanced way.

Composite Views

The software program on the CD-ROM has been specially designed to help you with this evaluation. It does not address all of the issues you will want to discuss in a thorough evaluation, but it will offer some fascinating perspectives that you can add to your evaluation. (For some additional issues to discuss, see Worksheet I: Bringing Balance to Your Church's Ministry Profile.)

The simplest part of the software program is the composite *Change Compass*. By entering the three final values from each member's *Change Compass* you can get a composite picture of your entire con- gregation (or should you wish to break it down further, your Bible Study group, your Sunday school class, sub-congregation, etc.).

The portion of the program that relates to the *Three Color Gift Test* is more complex. It offers four separate composite views of the spiritual gifts in your church. There is a complete gift "spread" view for both manifest and latent gifts, as well as a color "tendency" view for both manifest and latent gifts. The "gift spread" allows you to see the exact scoring of all the manifest and latent gifts in your church. The "tendency" view simply brings all the gifts in your church together to show whether they lie more in the blue, green, or red areas.

How Should The Change Compass "Color" Your Implementation?

Once you have calculated your church's composite *Change Compass* results, your Implementation Team will have some additional information to consider at this point in the process for modifying your implementation strategy. Does your church as a whole have an affinity for one of the three key terms: power, wisdom, or commitment? Is there a deficiency in one of these areas? What would be some of the practical ministry consequences of an entire church that did its ministry with that strength and that deficiency? Do you believe this to be the case with your church? Why do you believe your church shows these tendencies?

Consider if these tendencies have already been addressed on a personal level in seminars, small groups, and one-on-one gift counseling. If they have been, you may not need to take any special measures at the church level. On the other hand, it is possible that there are some deeply embedded spiritual, philosophical, or structural dynamics in the church that will consistently generate similar results if not dealt with. What should you do about these?

In the following paragraphs you will find some suggestions about ways you could proceed with different composite *Change Compass* results. Keep in mind that for each of the three areas it can be helpful to consider measures for both initial and on-going growth. Here are some of the possible ways that a deficiency in a particular color might shape the way your team goes about its work.

Does your church as a whole have an affinity for one of the three key terms: power, wisdom, or commitment? Is there a deficiency in one of these areas?

Blue Deficiency Issues: "Discovery" and "Dependence"

Suppose your church scores low in the "power" area. How might this affect your implementation priorities?

Think of power in two ways: First, in terms of enablement that has been given. Second, in terms of further enablement that is available. The first of these relates to the Spirit's initial empowering of a believer for ministry, mostly by means of the spiritual gifts that have been given. The second relates more to special empowerment for a particular moment. Is a ministry exercised in conscious dependence upon God? Both of these orientations relate to enablement by God, but in one case it has to do with the discovery of gifts, and in the other with active dependence in the exercise of those gifts.

You may consider implementing measures aimed at both concerns. Is your church low in "power" for lack of knowing what their gifts are, or from a lack of on-going dependence in the exercise of ministry?

Green Deficiency Issues: "Training" and "Planning"

In a similar way, if "wisdom" scores lowest, you may wish to consider if the initial or the on-going aspect is more at issue. Perhaps you should plan for both.

If you give priority to the initial aspect, you may want to focus on offering training for the exercise of your members' gifts in their ministries. For example, offer a teacher training seminar for those with the gift of teaching. On the other hand, your teachers may already know plenty of teaching techniques, but are not adequately applying what they know. In that case you may wish to find a way to encourage regular planning and preparation. In well-run schools, for example, teachers submit a weekly lesson plan. This kind of low-key "oversight," might help your teachers consistently apply what they already know. Sure it may mean a little more work, but the benefits might well outweigh the effort both in terms of improved teaching for those who are taught and greater personal satisfaction for those who teach.

It can be helpful to consider measures for both initial and on-going growth in these areas.

Red Deficiency Issues: "Involvement" and "Consistency"

Should "commitment" score the lowest, you may wish to consider whether this has more to do with the involvement of your members in ministries that correspond with their gifts; or whether once involved in gift-oriented ministries, they are as consistent as they should be. Perhaps both situations occur in the church.

Design implementation steps that keep both of these possibilities in mind. Gift counseling, for example, can be very helpful for linking people with a good ministry. However, unless structured with regular "follow-up" appointments, it may not be the best option for assessing on-going growth and commitment. Therefore, you may wish, for instance, to have periodic ministry leaders' meetings to discuss the participation level of those in their ministries. How is it going? Are there some who seem to be only half-heartedly involved? What can be done to encourage them to a greater level of contribution?

(For a worksheet that might help you in the evaluation of your church's composite *Change Compass*, see Worksheet F: Evaluating Your Church's *Change Compass*.)

How Should The Gift Test "Color" Your Implementation?

Using the composite results of the *Three-Color Gift Test* may not be as straightforward as using the *Change Compass*. This is partially due to the greater complexity of the tool (four views), and partially due to underlying theological and philosophy of ministry considerations. For these reasons, your team will need to give careful consideration as to how you approach this subject.

For example, is your church theologically prepared to pursue all of the gifts discussed in *The 3 Colors of Ministry*? Have you modified the list at all in light of your theological convictions? And as to ministry philosophy, are you prepared to create new ministries should gifts be discovered in areas where you currently have nothing? Imagine that a church with no social outreach discovers that there are many untapped gifts in the "green" area. Are you willing to create such ministries, or, in light of your church's mission priorities, would you rather stick to channeling those gifts in ways that enhance existing ministries?

Hopefully your church already dealt with these fundamental issues to some extent before moving too far down the implementation path. However, a certain kind of reflection on these issues will only be possible once you can actually see what the distribution of gifts in your church really is. Therefore, consciously plan to wrestle with these issues now that this data is available to your Implementation Team.

Manifest Gift Distribution and Tendencies

Start with the actual distribution of gifts represented in your church. These are less interpretive because specific gifts have already been confirmed. Then move to the gift tendencies, which are more interpretive in the sense that categorizing gifts as "blue," "green," or "red," although logical is, nevertheless, a subjective categorization based on varying criteria, (see pages 102, 113, and 124 of *The 3 Colors of Ministry* for the specific criteria used). If the categorization criteria is kept clearly in mind, the tendency graph can also be a highly valuable look at your church.

Manifest Gift Distribution: Do you see any patterns? Are some gifts heavily represented while others are virtually absent? Why is this? Do some gifts tend to score higher than others? Why do you think this is? Do you have ministries that will utilize all the gifts represented? Why or why not? Take note of any item that catches your team's attention.

Manifest Gift Tendency: How are your church's manifest gifts distributed according to the three color categorization? Given what you know of the criteria used for this categorization, does this distribution surprise you? Why or why not?

(For a worksheet that might help you in the evaluation of the two composite manifest gift graphs, see Worksheet G: Evaluating Your Church's Manifest Gifts.)

Are you prepared to create new ministries should gifts be discovered in areas where you currently have nothing?

Latent Gift Distribution and Tendencies

Proceed in a similar manner with the two views for your church's latent gifts. Keep in mind that latent gifts indicate "possibilities." These are gifts that may exist in your church, but still need to be tested and confirmed. Nevertheless, latent gifts may also lie in the region of "solutions." Should your manifest gift distribution reveal areas where gifts are underrepresented or missing, and your latent gift distribution shows that your congregation may indeed have gifts in these areas, you may have an indication of some areas in which to focus future gift development.

Latent Gift Distribution: Do you see any patterns? Are some gifts heavily represented while others are virtually absent? Do some gifts tend to score higher than others? Are there ministries in which these gifts might be trained? Take note of any item that catches your team's attention.

Latent Gift Tendency: How are your church's latent gifts distributed according to the three-color categorization? Given what you know of the criteria used for this categorization, does this distribution surprise you? Why or why not?

(For a worksheet that might help you in the evaluation of the two composite latent gift graphs, see Worksheet H: Evaluating Your Church's Latent Gifts.)

> *The purpose of these evaluations is to see if there are any ways in which you need to modify your implementation strategy at this point in the process in order to achieve greater balance in your church's ministry long term.*

Seek Greater Balance Through Mid-Course Corrections

The purpose of these evaluations is to see if there are any ways in which you need to modify your implementation strategy, at this point in the process, in order to achieve greater balance in your church's ministry long term. If your team should discover any needed modifications, have the courage to address those needs and introduce them into your on-going implementation strategy.

It would be a shame if, after having done so much work to make the ministry of your church more gift-oriented, it suffered from some imbalance in either the way it does ministry or in what ministry it does. A mid-course correction at this point might open up new possibilities for service and preclude problems down the road.

Inside and Outside the Church

Another way to pursue greater balance in your ministry is to make certain that your ministry profile does not focus exclusively on ministries within the church. There's a whole world outside the walls of every local congregation. God's desire is that the gifts which he has given to the church demonstrate his character outside of the church as well.

Sometimes churches have an imbalance in their outward ministry, due to the fact that their engagement with the world is only conceived of in certain predefined ways, handed to them by their ecclesiastical tradition. Thinking "outside the box" could prove a very interesting and profitable activity.

(For a worksheet that might help you in the evaluation of your ministries inside and outside the church, see Worksheet K: Enhancing Balance Inside and Outside the Church.)

Largely red outside: For example, many churches' engagement with the world is predominantly, if not exclusively, evangelistic (red area). These churches might find it interesting to ask, "What if we were to use the wonderful 'green' gifts that God has placed in our church for the benefit of those who do not have a relationship with Christ?" "Perhaps some of our members with gifts of hospitality (green area) could open their homes to visiting family members of inmates in our nearby prison."

Largely green outside: Other churches might find that their engagement with the world is strictly "green." Maybe your church could profitably investigate if it can use gifts in the blue area for the benefit of those outside the church. Some churches, for instance, have prayer-walking ministries that regularly intercede for the concerns of non-Christians they meet on the street. Not only is such prayer generally appreciated, often it has led to people finding their way to Christ.

Largely blue outside: Maybe yours is a very "blue" church when it comes to the way you relate to those outside the church body. Is it possible that God might have some other ministries for you? Have you identified any members in your church with the gift of counseling (red area)? Perhaps you could offer emotional or financial counseling to members of the community.

Another way to pursue greater balance in your ministry is to make certain that your ministry profile does not focus exclusively on ministries within the church.

Obviously, the purpose in this evaluation is not to create ministries for the sake of creating ministries. It is simply another way to ask the question, "How does *God* want to organize the ministry of this local congregation?" The gift-oriented approach begins with the assumption that God's ideal organization relates to the spiritual gifts he has given, and this last line of thought simply asks if more of those gifts should be directed to needs outside the church.

Not every church needs to do every ministry. There is only so much that any congregation can be involved in at one time. However, that which is defined as the limits of what a local congregation can get involved in, is frequently determined, not by the gifting of the members of the congregation, but by some pre-established ministry blueprint. This blueprint is often defined by the denominational hierarchy, or perhaps even the pastor's gifting, but not by the spiritual gifts that God has granted the congregation.

Once the gift-oriented ministry approach is fully implemented, most churches will discover that the church is capable of doing far more ministry than it has done up to the present time. Such an assertion is based on at least two observations. The first is that in most churches, only a small portion of the members are serving in any ministry. The second is that not all of those who are serving in a ministry are doing so in ways that correspond with their gifting. If these two observations are accurate, an increase in the level of gift-oriented ministry involvement should also produce an increase in the quality of ministry a church is able to do. First, because more people will be involved. Second, because, by serving in the area of their gifting, they will produce at a higher, more effective level.

Step 9:
Maintain Your Momentum

M ost churches like the gift-oriented approach to ministry. Yet few of them take concrete steps towards the practical implementation of this approach. Everyone begins the implementation process with good intentions to follow through. The following checklist can help you follow through by helping you to see what you have accomplished and what is yet to be done.

Go through this list on a regular basis and check off all the steps your church has already taken. Since this is a process, you will not be able to check many items off at any one time. However, you should be able to check off at least one item each month, though it is not necessary to follow the steps in the order in which they are listed.

Check list

- ❑ The church leadership fully supports the implementation of the gift-oriented approach to ministry.
- ❑ The church leadership has gone through *The 3 Colors of Ministry* in either a small group or seminar format.
- ❑ A Ministry Coordinator has been selected.
- ❑ The small group and ministry leaders have gone through a small group experience using *The 3 Colors of Ministry*.
- ❑ The Ministry Coordinator has formed a team.
- ❑ A full list of actual and potential church tasks has been developed.
- ❑ A ministry description has been written for each church ministry, both actual and potential.
- ❑ There is consistent teaching on the discovery and use of spiritual gifts in the church.
- ❑ At least 75% of the church's small groups have studied *The 3 Colors of Ministry* in detail.
- ❑ At least 75% of church attenders have identified their gifts.
- ❑ At least 75% of the members who know what their spiritual gifts are have also found a corresponding task within the church.
- ❑ The church leadership knows which church members have which spiritual gifts.
- ❑ A summary of the manifest and latent spiritual gifts in the church (composite Gift Distribution) is available.
- ❑ The church's composite *Change Compass* has been evaluated.
- ❑ Needed mid-course corrections have been made to the implementation strategy to ensure greater balance in ministry.
- ❑ Volunteers are regularly encouraged to leave tasks or ministries that do not correspond to their spiritual gifting.

❑ There is one person (maybe even several people) whose main task is to continuously coordinate spiritual gifts and the tasks/ministries in the church.

❑ The gift counselors have various support tools (i.e., list of available ministries, up-to-date ministry descriptions, gift-counselor training, etc.) at their disposal.

❑ Every member who has identified his or her spiritual gift(s) has had at least one gift-counseling session to discuss his or her calling.

❑ Everyone who joins the church is assisted in the discovery of his or her spiritual gifts and is using them for the honor of God and the edification of the body.

❑ Christians regularly share testimonies in church meetings as to how God has blessed them as they have applied their spiritual gifts.

❑ The pastor's ministry is focused on those tasks for which God has gifted him or her.

❑ There are plenty of ministry opportunities for every individual to be able to experiment with his or her spiritual gifts.

❑ The church regularly provides training events and instruction on the various spiritual gifts.

❑ Each volunteer is coached by, and responsible to a contact person (i.e. "ministry department director").

❑ Ways have been found to use most spiritual gifts to meet the needs of non-Christians.

❑ Progress in becoming a gift-oriented church is regularly evaluated.

❑ Members are encouraged to test their gifts from time to time.

❑ There is an environment in the church that facilitates experimenting with spiritual gifts.

❑ The church not only addresses spiritual gifts, but also the "fruit of the Spirit" (Gal. 5:22).

❑ The results of the process are checked regularly.

❑ A date has been set for carrying out an NCD profile of the church in order to evaluate the quality characteristic "Gift-oriented Ministry," and see what progress has been made.

Checklists, Worksheets, and Reference Information

On the following pages you will find a number of resources aimed at helping you put balanced, gift-oriented ministry to work in your church. You can use these tools "as is" or as guides for creating your own personalized tools. In either case you should find them a valuable aid to your efforts.

Worksheet A: Gaining the Support of Your Leaders

Whose support do you need?

1. _____
2. _____
3. _____
4. _____
5. _____

6. _____
7. _____
8. _____
9. _____
10. _____

Why should they get behind a gift-oriented ministry process?

1. What needs in the church would encourage these leaders to support this process?

2. What kinds of expectations do you have for this process? Are they realistic?

3. If this process achieved its goal, what would the church look like in two years?

4. What concerns or preconceived notions exist that might hinder support for this process? (Do you truly understand and appreciate these concerns?)

5. In what ways could you meaningfully involve the leaders in this process?

6. Do you need to develop a better relationship with any of the "opinion makers" in the church?

7. Will you seek the coaching of an outside consultant? If so, who?

How should they experience the process?

1. When will you take your key leaders through a "pilot" experience with *The 3 Colors of Ministry*?

2. Jot some notes below as to how you will structure this experience.

(a) What format will you use? (regular leadership meetings, separate weekly or biweekly-meetings, weekend course, other?)

(b) How much of the material will you cover? (12, 6, 3, or 1-week program, other?)

Worksheet B: Structuring Your Implementation Team

Goals:	Date:
Work-flow	

Ministry Coordinator / Phone #	Spiritual Gifts / Responsibilities

Gift Counselors / Phone #	Spiritual Gifts / Responsibilities

Seminar or Study Leaders / Phone #	Spiritual Gifts / Responsibilities

Ministry Assistants / Phone #	Spiritual Gifts / Responsibilities

Worksheet C: Defining Ministries and their Descriptions

What are the ministries of your church?

1. Do you have a church ministry organization chart? If so, is it complete and up-to-date?

2. If it is not complete and up-to-date, who will be responsible to make sure that it is? When will they do this?

(As you expand the ministry organization chart, you might seek to do this in ways that will allow for future development. Perhaps create a general, "bird's-eye" view of the church's ministries with more detailed supporting charts for each ministry area. Developing a "flexible" chart is also a good idea. Such a chart will not only allow for the possibility that your church's ministry will grow in depth and breadth, but it could also form the basis of an "intuitive" filing system so that the day-to-day tasks of maintaining or updating information can be done without difficulty.)

How will you go about creating all of the necessary ministry descriptions?

1. When will you meet with the appropriate leaders to "flesh-out" the ministry organization chart with a list of specific tasks and responsibilities? Will you meet with everyone at once, or will you have several meetings with different people, covering a different ministry area at each meeting?

2. Will you develop ministry descriptions in those meetings, or will you ask ministry leaders to bring completed ministry descriptions with them? (Be sure that you make copies of Worksheet E available.)

3. Will you invite your gift counselors to these meetings? If you don't plan to invite them (or if you simply don't have any gift counselors yet), how do you plan to make sure that they have a thorough grasp of all of the specific ministry tasks that are available?

4. How will you keep the church's ministry descriptions current? What sort of procedure will you put in place to make sure that old ministry descriptions are removed, new ones are added, and changed ministry descriptions are updated?

Worksheet D: Conducting a Task Analysis

If you are not sure what spiritual gifts are needed for a specific task or ministry, perform a "task analysis." This enables you to look at every task in terms of the spiritual gifts necessary.

With your group of leaders, apply the task analysis question-naire (pages 62 and 63) to each responsibility or ministry that you want to analyze. Work through the 60 statements together, determining to what degree the respective statement applies in each case. Discuss each statement together and allow enough time to answer all of the questions.

Step 1: In the small boxes on the evaluation chart, enter the values you marked for each question (0 = never, 1 = rarely, 2 = sometimes, 3 = often, 4 = very often).

Step 2: Add the two digits that appear next to each other on the table (that is, the numerical values of questions 1 and 31, questions 2 and 32, and so on) and enter their sum to the right under "Total for Gift."

Step 3: Identify the five highest scores in the "Total for Gift" column. Write the names of the corresponding spiritual gifts below. (If two values are the same, it does not matter what spiritual gift you enter first.)

Name of the task: _____

Spiritual gifts needed:

1. _____

2. _____

3. _____

4. _____

5. _____

The spiritual gifts listed here are the ones most needed in order to accomplish the analyzed task. Include these spiritual gifts in the corresponding ministry description and only choose volunteers for this task whose spiritual gift mix includes at least one or more of these spiritual gifts.

* Pay special attention to the gifts with an asterisk. These gifts are understood differently from group to group. See Chapter 5 of *The 3 Colors of Ministry* for the definitions upon which this gift test has been developed.

Evaluation Chart		Total for Gift
1	31	Organization
2	32	Missionary*
3	33	Singleness
4	34	Discernment
5	35	Evangelism
6	36	Counseling
7	37	Faith
8	38	Giving
9	39	Deliverance
10	40	Healing
11	41	Teaching
12	42	Tongues*
13	43	Wisdom*
14	44	Voluntary poverty
15	45	Craftsmanship
16	46	Helps
17	47	Hospitality
18	48	Prayer
19	49	Interpretation
20	50	Knowledge*
21	51	Leadership
22	52	Suffering
23	53	Mercy
24	54	Miracles
25	55	Apostle*
26	56	Shepherding*
27	57	Prophecy*
28	58	Service
29	59	Music
30	60	Artistic creativity

Task Analysis Questionnaire

Task to be analyzed: _____

This task *(4) very often, (3) often, (2) sometimes, (1) rarely (0) never* **requires the ability to ...**

1	... develop detailed plans for accomplishing certain goals.
2	... integrate into another culture and adapt to foreign customs.
3	... live without a spouse and family.
4	... evaluate statements made by others to determine whether they might mislead the church.
5	... talk with non-Christians about Jesus and one's relationship to him.
6	... encourage others.
7	... formulate goals that appear unrealistic to others and pursue them in a systematic manner.
8	... generously share one's money and possessions for the expansion of the kingdom of God.
9	... play a role in delivering others from demonic influence.
10	... pray regularly for the healing of the sick.
11	... work on materials that will help others learn in a simple and interesting way.
12	... pray in tongues.
13	... help others analyze their situation.
14	... stick to a modest standard of living.
15	... repair and maintain things.
16	... work in the background to support others who are in a more visible ministry.
17	... welcome even unexpected guests and provide them with food and lodging.
18	... spend much time in prayer.
19	... hear what God wants to communicate when others speak in tongues.
20	... spend a lot of time studying in order to gain new insights.
21	... lead people in such a way that they learn to work together toward a common goal.
22	... demonstrate a positive mindset in the midst of suffering and pain.
23	... care for those who are on the fringe of society.
24	... pray for the supernatural.
25	... solve problems in other churches.
26	... care for the spiritual well-being of others and mentor them in their spiritual journey.
27	... serve as God's channel for giving clear direction in concrete situations.
28	... assume minor and seemingly unimportant responsibilities in the church.
29	... work hard to develop one's musical abilities.
30	... express one's thoughts and feelings through the arts (drama, pantomime, painting, etc.).

Task to be analyzed: _____

This task *(4) very often, (3) often, (2) sometimes, (1) rarely (0) never* **requires the ability to ...**

31	... manage business or organizational projects independently.
32	... establish contact with those who have a completely different life-style than oneself.
33	... deny oneself the possibility of establishing a family.
34	... determine whether another person's words are of divine, human, or satanic origin.
35	... sense when another person is open to the Gospel.
36	... quickly take a conversation with someone one hardly knows to a more meaningful level.
37	... pray and work toward something that other Christians would consider impossible.
38	... regularly give a significant amount of one's resources for the furthering of the kingdom.
39	... recognize whether there are areas of someone's life that are under demonic influence.
40	... pray for the sick in a personal and concrete way.
41	... share insights and information in a logical, interesting, and easily-understandable way.
42	... publicly pray or speak words inspired by God, through the medium of tongues.
43	... apply theoretical knowledge to a concrete situation.
44	... maintain a low standard of living.
45	... resolve technical problems that normally demand a repairman.
46	... assist other Christians in their work so that they can be more effective in their ministry.
47	... help visitors feel "at home."
48	... pray intensively over a period of weeks or months for certain concerns.
49	... sense what God wants to say when someone is speaking in tongues.
50	... discover, formulate, and systematize ideas that are important for the health of a church.
51	... delegate tasks to others.
52	... accept suffering for the cause of Christ.
53	... express sympathy toward others who are in need.
54	... pray for signs and wonders.
55	... counsel groups and churches with regard to their spiritual situation.
56	... mentor a group of Christians and to work toward their unity.
57	... receive insights from God reflecting his will in specific situations.
58	... involve oneself in tasks that others regard as less attractive.
59	... learn a musical instrument.
60	... exercise creative forms of communication such as painting, drama, and pantomime.

Chapter 4:
Support Material

Worksheet E:
Ministry Description

Task	Date

Goals

Sub-tasks

Contact people
Responsible for:
Responsible to:
Work with:

Spiritual gifts	Abilities/Interests

Time commitment	Length of assignment

Training

Additional agreements

Worksheet F: Evaluating Your Church's Change Compass

Date: _____

How did your church score in ...?

Power: _____ (Total A)

Wisdom: _____ (Total B)

Commitment: _____ (Total C)

Graph your composite results on the chart to the right.

Total B

15
10
5

5   5
10   10
15   15
Total A   Total C

Interpreting the Results

1. How would you interpret the results of this composite *Change Compass*?

2. How, if at all, should this interpretation "color" your implementation efforts? (Would any of the suggestions given for individual believers under "Next Steps" on pages 38-40 of *The 3 Colors of Ministry* be at all suggestive for your church? If so, which ones, and how would they apply at the whole church level?)

3. List several ways in which your church could grow in those areas that seem to be under-developed right now.

4. What relationship, if any, would you identify between the "color blend" of your church's ministry style (composite *Change Compass*) and the gifts being employed in your church (Manifest Gift Tendency) or future areas of potential gift usage (Latent Gift Tendency)?

Worksheet G: Evaluating Your Church's Manifest Gifts

Date: _____

Manifest Gift Tendency

How did your church score in each area?

Blue: _____ Green: _____ Red: _____

Sketch your church's manifest gift tendency. How would you interpret these results?

"Green" Gifts

"Blue" Gifts   "Red" Gifts

How, if at all, should this interpretation "color" your implementation efforts?

Manifest Gift Distribution

What gifts appeared most frequently?

How does this "color" the way your church ministers?

Which gifts appeared infrequently or not at all?

How would you explain this? (Theological convictions? Teaching Emphases? The Holy Spirit's sovereign distribution of gifts?)

Worksheet H: Evaluating Your Church's Latent Gifts

Date: _____

Latent Gift Tendency

How did your church score in each area?

Blue: _____ **Green:** _____ **Red:** _____

Sketch your church's latent gift tendency. How would you interpret these results?

"Green" Gifts

"Blue" Gifts   "Red" Gifts

How, if at all, should this interpretation "color" your implementation efforts?

Latent Gift Distribution

What gifts appeared most frequently?

What, if anything, should your church do in response to this? (Initiate training in these areas? Give more teaching on these subjects?)

Did any gifts not appear at all?

What explanation would you give for this?

Worksheet I: Bringing Balance to Your Church's Ministry Profile

Distribution of Ministries

1. Does your church have ministries in each of the three general categories? Are they somewhat evenly distributed? Do you believe they should be? Why or why not?

2. Are there areas in which you have gifts, but no ministries? In what areas? What untapped gifts do you have that could be dedicated to new ministries in those areas?

3. Are there areas in which you have ministries, but no gifts? What areas? What should you do about these ministries?

Development of Ministries

1. How could you develop new ministries in areas that are currently under-developed?

2. Would you need to modify your church's mission statement at all if you added ministries in these areas?

3. Consider a ministry "brainstorming" task force. Take an area of potential ministry that you would like to explore. Who has gifts in that area that you could invite to be on such a brainstorming team?

Modification of Ministries

1. Can you think of ways in which existing ministries can be made more balanced?

2. Are there unused gifts (or latent gifts) in your church that could be incorporated into existing ministries in a way that would add new, previously unconsidered possibilities for those ministries? How?

Worksheet J: Sub-Category Exploration

Green Area	Use in existing ministries	Potential new ministries
Social needs		
Human mind		
Creative potential		

Red Area	Use in existing ministries	Potential new ministries
Sharing the gospel		
Leadership		
Assistance		

Blue Area	Use in existing ministries	Potential new ministries
Uncompromis-ing trust		
Communicating God's messages		
God's supernatural power		

Chapter 4:
Support Material

Worksheet K: Enhancing Balance "Inside" and "Outside" the Church

A pproximately what percentage of the ministries of your church are internally focused? Approximately what percentage are focused outside? Is this a ratio with which you are satisfied?

If you believe that you need to enhance the ministry balance of your church, spend some time brainstorming in light of the following areas:

"Green" Gift Ministries Inside	"Green" Gift Ministries Outside
"Red" Gift Ministries Inside	**"Red" Gift Ministries Outside**
"Blue" Gift Ministries Inside	**"Blue" Gift Ministries Outside**

Appendix A: Tasks and Corresponding Spiritual Gifts

The following list is intended to help you as you match spiritual gifts with ministries in your church. Of course, this list is not comprehensive. Nor may you find all of the ministries of your church mentioned. However, if you do find a task or ministry that your church already has, it is not necessary to do a task analysis for that task or ministry. Save yourself some time!

To qualify for the task or ministry under consideration, a volunteer must have one, several, or all of the spiritual gifts mentioned.

Babysitting / Child Care
Service
Shepherding

Bible Study Leader
Teaching
Wisdom

Child Evangelism
Evangelism
Shepherding

Choir Director
Music
Leadership

Choir Member
Music

Church Bulletin Editor
Organization
Artistic Creativity

Church Board Member
Faith
Leadership
Discernment
Wisdom

Church Consulting
Apostle
Wisdom

Church Development Research
Knowledge

Church Development Training
Teaching

Church Leadership
Faith
Leadership
Wisdom

Church-Planting Team Member
Evangelism
Shepherding
Organization
Helps
Prayer

Church-Planting Vocation
Apostle
Singleness
Leadership
Missionary
Evangelism

Cleaning
Service

Community Service
Craftsmanship
Helps
Service

Computer-Related Tasks
Organization
Helps

Conference, Seminar Coordination
Organization

Conflict Resolution
Wisdom
Counseling

Construction
Craftsmanship

Cooking and Baking
Service

Counseling Ministry
Mercy
Deliverance
Evangelism
Healing
Prophecy
Counseling
Discernment
Wisdom

Crafts
Artistic creativity

Creative Evangelism
Knowledge
Artistic creativity
Music
Evangelism

Cross-Cultural Ministry, at Home or Abroad
Apostle
Mercy
Deliverance
Singleness
Evangelism
Voluntary poverty
Leadership
Craftmanship
Suffering
Missionary
Prophecy
Miracles

Disaster Relief
Giving
Service

Drama Group
Artistic creativity
Music

Drug Advisory Center
Counseling
Mercy

Drug Rehabilitation
Mercy
Evangelism
Counseling

Evangelism
Deliverance
Evangelism
Leadership
Prophecy
Discernment
Prayer

Exorcism
Deliverance
Prayer
Counseling
Discernment
Evangelism

Family Counseling
Counseling

Fellowship/Interpersonal Relationships
Hospitality

Finance Committee
Giving
Organization

Financial Supporter
Giving

Gardening
Service
Craftsmanship
Artistic Creativity

Gift Counselor
Wisdom
Organization
Counseling
Discernment
Teaching

Homeless Ministry
Mercy
Hospitality
Evangelism

Homeless Shelter
Mercy
Voluntary poverty
Evangelism

Hospitality Service
Service
Hospitality

Intercession
Mercy
Prayer
Suffering
Healing
Discernment
Faith
Miracles

Interdenominational Ministries
Apostle
Wisdom

Interior Design
Artistic creativity

Janitor
Service

Leadership Support
Helps

Librarian
Organization

Lodging
Hospitality

Long-term Planning
Apostle
Knowledge
Leadership
Organization
Prophecy
Discernment

Maintenance
Craftsmanship

Manual Labors
Service
Craftsmanship

Marginalized, Ministry to the
Mercy
Deliverance
Evangelism
Voluntary poverty
Hospitality

Missionary
Counseling
Discernment

Mercy Ministry
Mercy
Evangelism
Voluntary poverty

Mime
Artistic creativity

Ministry Coordinator
Leadership
Organization

Ministry Leader
Leadership
Organization

Music Group
Music

Music Ministries (e.g. Band, ...)
Evangelism
Music
Artistic Creativity

New Believer Care
Shepherding
Counseling

New Believer Classes
Teaching

Newsletter Editor
Artistic creativity
Organization

Office Staff
Helps
Organization

"Open" Small Group
Evangelism
Leadership
Teaching

Pastor
Faith
Leadership
Shepherding

Personal Counseling
Counseling
Wisdom

Physically Disabled, Ministry to the
Mercy
Shepherding
Evangelism

Pick-up service
Service

Pioneer Work
Apostle
Suffering
Leadership
Prayer
Faith
Evangelism

Prayer Chain Ministry
Prayer
Faith

Prayer Group Leader
Prayer
Faith
Leadership

Prayer Group Member
Interpretation
Prayer
Prophecy
Discernment
Tongues
Miracles
Healing
Deliverance

Prayer Meeting Leader
Prayer
Leadership

Prayer Ministry
Deliverance
Prayer
Healing
Prophecy
Counseling
Discernment

Wisdom
Tongues
Interpretation

Preaching
Evangelism
Teaching
Discernment
Wisdom

Prison Ministry
Mercy
Evangelism
Counseling

Profiling Churches
Knowledge
Apostle

Public Relations
Knowledge
Prophecy
Discernment

Publicity
Artistic creativity

Radio Ministry
Evangelism

Receptionist
Helps
Organization

Relocation Ministry
Helps
Organization

Retreat Coordinator
Hospitality
Leadership
Organization

Seminar Teacher
Knowledge
Teaching
Wisdom

Seniors Ministry
Shepherding
Counseling

Single Parent Ministry
Mercy
Counseling

Small Group Coordinator
Organization

Small Group Host
Hospitality

Small group Leader
Shepherding
Teaching

Social Coordinator
Organization

Soloist
Music

Songwriting and Composition
Artistic creativity
Music

Special Events
Evangelism
Leadership

Spiritual Warfare
Interpretation
Prayer
Miracles
Tongues
Deliverance

Sunday School
Shepherding
Teaching

Tape Ministry
Service

Typing Manuscripts
Service
Helps

Treasurer
Giving
Organization

Teaching and Training
Teaching
Wisdom

Street Ministry
Evangelism
Artistic creativity
Music

Telephone Counseling
Counseling
Wisdom

Terminally Ill Care
Counseling
Wisdom
Mercy

Vision Team
Faith

Visitation
Compassion
Healing
Music
Counseling
Evangelism

Volunteer Training
Shepherding
Teaching

Welcome Committee
Hospitality

Worship Leader
Music
Leadership

Worship Service Planning Committee
Prayer
Artistic creativity
Music
Prophecy

Worship Team Member
Music

Writing
Artistic Creativity
Knowledge
Teaching
Wisdom

Youth Ministry
Hospitality
Shepherding

Appendix B: Using The 3 Colors of Ministry CD-ROM

The CD-ROM that accompanies this book contains a number of items designed to assist you in the implementation process. Following is a descriptive list, along with a few technical notes that will help you get the most out of each tool.

Basic Functionality

When you access *The 3 Colors of Ministry* CD-ROM you will notice several folders. Double-click on the folder that you wish to access.

Each folder contains content that can either be used straight from the CD or copied to your hard disk. The only exception to this is the folder labeled "3CSoft." It contains the composite *Change Compass* and *Three-Color Gift Test* software, and *must* be copied to your hard drive in order to be used.

The "3CSoft" Folder

In this folder you will find several files. Among them is the program file, which is labeled 3CQC2.exe. Copy this file, and *all* the other files in the folder to the subdirectory of your choice on your computer's hard drive. Once you have done this, double click on the file labeled NCDRegister.bat to properly configure the program with Windows. Then, simply double click on the 3CQC2.exe icon (the icon with the three-colors symbol) to launch the program. (3CQC2 stands for "3 Colors Quality Characteristic 2") You might also want to open the Readme.txt file to see if there are any other installation or usage instructions you should know about.

The software's start-up screen will offer you several language choices. Choose the language you wish to use, and you will be taken to the main screen, where you can select one of three spreadsheet folders with which to work.

The software's start-up screen will offer you several language choices. Choose the language you wish to use, and you will be taken to the main screen, where you can select one of three spreadsheet folders with which to work.

The first folder is titled, "Composite Change Compass." Click here if you wish to input the results of the *Change Compass* of a small group, an adult Sunday school class, or your entire church. Type in the name of the person and their totals for Columns A, B, and C. Be sure to click on the "Save" button when you are finished. Once you have done this, click on the "View" button to see the composite result.

The other two tabs work similarly. They are labeled "Composite Manifest Gifts" and "Composite Latent Gifts." Select the one you wish to use, and type in the corresponding results from your church members' *Three-Color Gift Test* answer sheets (see "Understanding the results," page 85 of *The 3 Colors of Ministry*).

Type in the name of the person whose results you're inputting and then enter the spiritual gifts that scored highest in each category (manifest or latent) and the values that each gift received (These *must* be values between 70 and 130). Space is provided for up to five gifts per person in each category, but you are not obligated to enter five. You can enter four, three, two, or even just one. Be sure to click on the "Save" button when you have finished entering in the data.

In addition to program updates, the site also features downloadable worksheets, information on the status of other 3 Colors resources, and other items of interest.

To view the composite results, click one of the two buttons that appears at the bottom of the screen. "View Spread" gives you the distribution of the spiritual gifts in your church. In this graph, each gift is plotted with a dot according to it's score on the test. The "View Tendency" button presents you with a view that is similar to that of the *Change Compass*. Here, however, it is a representation of whether the spiritual gifts in your church lie more in one color area or another.

Once you have entered all of the data and viewed the results, it is time to work with the insights you have gained. To do this, "Step 8: Pursue Greater Balance in Your Church's Ministry Profile" (pages 48-54) and Worksheets F through K (pages 65-70) will be particularly helpful.

Should you wish to remove the software from your computer, simply double click on the file titled "NCDRemove.bat", and all the software's files will be unregistered. Then, delete the contents of the folder you have placed the program in.

The NCD International 3CSoft Web Site

The Institute for Natural Church Development periodically plans to update the software found on the CD-ROMs that come with this book and others in the "3 Colors" series. In fact, due to publishing deadlines, we would urge you to drop by the site just as soon as you are ready to use the software to see if there is a newer version that has become available since the book's publishing date.

In addition to program updates, the site also features downloadable worksheets, information on the status of other 3 Colors resources, and other items of interest. The URL of the NCD International web page is: **www.ncd-international.org**

The "3CMGraphics" Folder

The "3CMGraphics" folder contains all of the original graphics from *The 3 Colors of Ministry*. Each image has been included in both a high resolution and low resolution TIF format. Open them in your favorite graphics program, and use them for making transparencies, printing color handouts, or preparing Power Point presentations.

The numbering system of the images corresponds to their page in *The 3 Colors of Ministry*. By refering to the page number in the book, you will know which file to select on the CD-ROM. If there is more than one graphic on a given page, a lower case letter ("a," "b," "c," etc.) follows the number. "H" and "L" stand for high and low resolution images, respectively. Thus, you will find TIF files with names like the following: H14, H16a, L16b, L23, etc.

The numbering system of the images corresponds to their page in The 3 Colors of Ministry.

The "3CMWorksheets" Folder

While you can easily photocopy the worksheets right out of the books, some people prefer to work directly with their own printers. For this reason, we have included the worksheets from the three *NCD Implementation Resources* for the Quality Characteristic, Gift-Oriented Ministry, in PDF format (Adobe Acrobat) on this disk. These are labeled exactly as they are in the books (Worksheet B, Worksheet J, etc), and are available in two formats: Letter (8½x11 in.) and A4 (210x297 mm.).

The "3foldArt" Folder

There is one other folder on the CD-ROM that does not correspond directly to the *NCD Implementation Resources* for the Quality Characteristic of Gift-Oriented Ministry. This folder is labeled "3foldArt" and contains the graphics from Christian Schwarz's book *The Threefold Art of Experiencing God*. Since the subject matter of that book is related to the approach taken in *The 3 Colors of Ministry*, we have included the graphics here for those readers who would find it useful.

Don't forget to visit the 3 Colors software site at:

www.ncd-international.org